JB JOSSEY-BASS™
A Wiley Brand

The Operational Plan

How to Create a Yearlong Membership Plan

Scott C. Stevenson, Editor

WILEY

The Operational Plan:
How to Create
A Yearlong Membership Plan

Published by

Stevenson, Inc.

P.O. Box 4528 • Sioux City, Iowa • 51104

Phone 712.239.3010 • Fax 712.239.2166

www.stevensoninc.com

The Operational Plan: How to Create a Yearlong Membership Plan

GETTING STARTED: EXAMINE HISTORICAL DATA, CONDUCT INTERNAL AUDIT

To know where to go and how to get there, it helps to know where you've been. That's why it's important to have a solid baseline of historical data that includes metrics for member renewal rates, new member acquisitions, retention rates, and more. Equally important is examining your internal preparedness to grow and to retain and better serve your members.

Operational Plans Have Seven Essential Elements

The most successful member organizations have a yearlong operational plan in place that serves as a road map for the upcoming fiscal year. Everyone who contributes to membership growth and development should be involved in creating or shaping the operational plan. The seven essential elements of an annual operational plan include:

1. Evaluating current membership programs and historical data.
2. Establishing membership goals for the upcoming year (e.g., overall increase in members, member retention, membership programs and more).
3. Setting quantifiable objectives that support those goals.
4. Designing action plans (individual strategies) that spell out how those objectives will be met (e.g., member recruitment campaigns, changes to existing procedures, etc.).
5. Creating a yearlong calendar that identifies the details of what needs to occur by when and who is responsible.
6. Monitoring the plan's progress throughout the year and making adjustments as needed.
7. Evaluating the plan at year-end in light of achievements and missed expectations.

Start by Evaluating Existing Programs

As you work to prepare an operational plan for the upcoming year — a plan that identifies goals, objectives, strategies, action plans and timetables — it's critical that you begin by evaluating what is currently being done and making changes based on the success (or lack of) of existing programs.

As a first step in the planning process, it will be enormously helpful if you can evaluate the current year in light of past years' results. Examples of historical review may include:

- Total membership numbers for the past several years.
- Member numbers within each membership category.
- Retention metrics over a period of years.
- Statistics regarding the composition of your membership each year for a period of years (e.g., age, gender, geographic location).
- Stats that evaluate member involvement in useful ways.

As you evaluate the existing year's programs in light of previous years' results, when possible, attempt to quantify each program in terms of: the cost-to-benefit ratio, the percentage of staff time and budget required to carry out each program and a comparison to other programs.

In addition, weigh each program in light of its long-versus short-term payoff. Some membership programs, for instance, may take years to achieve results, however, those results may far outweigh another program's benefits.

Depending on the type of nonprofit or association you represent, examples of individual programs or specific member benefits to be evaluated may include:

- Educational/professional development programs.
- Member affinity programs.
- Chapter programs.
- Events geared to members.

These program evaluation results will serve as your planning foundation.

Examine Why Members Leave

If you've had a sudden drop in membership, don't just blame it on the economy and fail to seek a solution. Rather, consider the possible reasons for the drop, then take action to reverse the trend.

Gather your membership committee and ask these questions to find solutions to the dip in membership:

- ❑ Do our members feel that meetings are useful, engaging?
- ❑ Does our nonprofit encourage diversity?
- ❑ Are members encouraged to speak at meetings and contribute to the greater good of our organization?
- ❑ Do members feel as though the organization's goals match their interests?
- ❑ Are members finding the meetings to be too time consuming?
- ❑ Do members feel rewarded and feel as though they benefit from membership?
- ❑ Has membership become cliquish, appearing to be open to only a select group? How can we overcome that?

Find answers to these questions by polling members, hosting a member retreat or creating a clearly defined survey as a first solid step to reducing member attrition.

GETTING STARTED: EXAMINE HISTORICAL DATA, CONDUCT INTERNAL AUDIT

Examine Data Before Setting Plans for Growth

Before setting membership growth goals, examine data relevant to your organization.

Important data to consider include historical and forecasted growth of the economy in the countries in which membership resides and the history of the organization.

"Oftentimes, much of this data isn't available, so a certain amount of guess work enters into membership goal setting," says Lee Anne Snedeker, senior vice president of membership and member analysis, The International Association of Business Communicators (IABC) in San Francisco, CA. "Accordingly, it (the data) should be revisited annually to test assumptions and review progress."

In addition, an organization needs to ensure it has the staffing and credibility to pursue its growth strategy, Snedeker says. "For example, expanding outside North America may look like an untapped growth opportunity, but does the organization have people in place within the targeted countries, are there resources to offer programming that's convenient and will large-scale translation efforts be necessary? Clearly, resources can be a challenge in some scenarios."

Beyond achieving a larger organization, there are other benefits to planning for growth. "If set correctly, membership growth goals can encourage the organization's staff to focus on a singular goal," Snedeker says. "Additionally, if there's a certain amount of stretch built into the goal, it encourages the team to aim high."

The results can be a bigger network — and more value — for your members.

Source: Lee Anne Snedeker, Senior Vice President, Membership and Member Analysis, The International Association of Business Communicators (IABC), San Francisco, CA. E-mail: lasnedeker@iabc.com

To Attract Members, Define Member Characteristics

If you're in the market to sign on new members, consider defining what a potential member for your nonprofit looks like to help determine where and when to make a membership pitch.

What characteristics would a potential member for your organization have?

Defining these potential member characteristics will also enable existing members, volunteers and staff to more readily identify a new member in the making.

Consider the following characteristics as possibilities:

❑ Nonmembers who are attending or have attended meetings. Be sure to capture the names and contact information of all who attend, so membership materials can be mailed to those who are not currently members.

❑ Persons who have inquired about membership and completed a member application but have not followed through with enrolling and paying membership dues. Don't let these potential members slip through the cracks — contact them today!

❑ College students or recent graduates. Make a presentation at a local college to recruit would-be members upon or prior to graduation. Getting young, new recruits can be a boon for your nonprofit and will assist the recent graduate as well.

❑ Employees of local firms. Seek out corporations within your community aligned with the practices of your membership. Offer a corporate group membership rate to any corporation enrolling 10 or more employees as new members.

❑ Persons seeking to pad their résumés. In today's tumultuous employment market, consider those potential members could benefit by acquiring new skills while they are unemployed as a member of your organization. Consider offering a special membership rate to those suffering a job loss.

❑ Members of complementary causes. Is there an organization in your community that is a natural fit to yours? Consider partnering with this organization to offer a dual membership that could conceivably bring hundreds more members your way.

To Grow Membership, Learn Why Current Members Joined

Effective target marketing requires that you know why people join your organization.

The Allegiance Research Group (ARG), Alexandria, VA, has a segmentation system called YTheyJoin that tells how members want to interact with an organization based on their current and future needs, which is different from data mining based on past behavior.

While the segmentation system is proprietary, ARG President Dale Paulson willingly shares his expertise about membership.

Paulson says that in the 1990s, ARG staff conducted dozens of membership surveys each year, and used this tool to determine why people joined. "Whenever money passes to someone else, there's always a reason. So we asked: Why did you write the check?"

They found nine reasons people joined. Paulson then used a fixed sum preference scale that measures preference and intensity to get a real picture of member categories.

Those member categories are:

1. **Mailboxers:** primarily want involvement through the mail, computer or mobile devices.

2. **Relevant Participants:** attend conventions and seminars, if relevant.

3. **Shapers:** stay most active and want to shape association policy.

4. **CompShoppers:** compare the association to other organizations or info/benefits.

5. **Cognoscenti:** want the association to add to their fund of knowledge.

6. **Boosters:** expect the association to improve their image.

7. **Altruistics:** share the values of the association and have interest in advocacy.

8. **Doubters:** tend to resist change and new initiatives.

9. **Non-relevants:** status has changed and association may not be relevant.

Paulson creates a pie chart of member categories for each association he works with to give them a good understanding of their membership. And while each pie chart is unique, some generalizations about segments can be made.

"We find CompShoppers, Doubters and Non-relevants are almost always the smallest categories," Paulson says. "The ones that fall in the middle tend to be Altruistics, Relevant Participants and Shapers. And the biggest categories are Mailboxers, Boosters and Cognoscenti."

Knowing why people join your organization allows you to develop targeted marketing programs for each category, which will allow you to spend money more efficiently, improve member services and increase retention, he says. For example, if you're looking for members to serve on committees or recruit new members, target Shapers. If you need members to participate in a letter-writing campaign to legislators, target Altruistics. Design different renewal letters and incentives based on the different needs of members.

Learn more at www.ytheyjoin.com.

Source: Dale Paulson, President, Allegiance Research Group, Alexandria, VA.
E-mail: allegianceresearch@gmail.com

Segmentation Ideas To Implement Today

If you don't have funds to hire a market research firm, you can still take steps to better understand your membership and target your marketing. Doing so begins with gathering and applying information, says Dale Paulson, president of Allegiance Research Group (Alexandria, VA) and author of the book, "Allegiance: Fulfilling the Promise of One-to-One Marketing for Associations."

"You're forming a partnership with members," says Paulson. "Say to them, 'You tell us what you want, and we'll make sure you get it.'"

To gather and apply member information to benefit your organization, Paulson says:

✓ **Look at your membership database and code it based on past behavior.** Does a member attend meetings? Buy tapes and publications? Serve on a committee?

✓ **Train your staff to be curious.** When someone joins, ask why and write it down. Every time a staffer answers the phone, have the person say, "For our records, we'd like to know what you expect from us. What can we provide for you?" And write it down. Even the receptionist should be asking, "Are you getting what you want?"

✓ **Always ask interactive questions.** Paulson remembers a story about New York City Mayor Ed Koch asking people around the city, "How are you?" The question invariably produced a monosyllabic, "Fine." When he changed his question to, "How am I doing?" New Yorkers unloaded on him, and he learned what he needed to know.

Learn From the Competition

■ To discover new and better ways of managing your organization and serving members, get on other member organizations' mailing lists. It's amazing what you can discover from reviewing others' materials.

Understand and Use Marketing Formulas

What is the value of a member? How much can I afford to spend to obtain a member? What is my membership retention rate?

When calculating the answers to these questions, Tony Rossell, senior vice president of Marketing General Incorporated. (Alexandria, VA) suggests using certain membership marketing formulas.

"For the most part, the membership marketing formulas are a shorthand way of calculating long standing economic performance measures in membership marketing. I have tried to outline simple, yet clear steps to calculate the numbers that are important benchmarks for membership organizations to know and use," he says.

Rossell has come up with four different marketing formulas and while it may seem complex, he says it's actually common sense. "If an organization loses 20 percent of its members each year, then it is common sense that "average tenure" or the average period of time for the entire membership to turn over is 5 years. Twenty percent is one fifth of 100 percent. Additionally, if a member pays $100 in dues and stays with an organization for 10 years, then the lifetime dues value of the member is $1,000," he says.

Rossell's marketing formulas are as follows:

Renewal Rate: Measures the number of members retained over a given period of time, usually during a fiscal or calendar year.

> *Total number of members today (minus 12 months of new members) / Total number of members in previous year*
>
> > *Example: (105 - 15)/100 = 90 percent Renewal Rate*

Average Tenure: How long, on average, do members stay with an association?

> *Reciprocal of Renewal Rate: 1 – Renewal Rate or, 1 - 0.90 = 0.10*
>
> > *Example: Divide Reciprocal into 1, or, 1 /.10 = an Average Tenure of 10 years*

Lifetime Value (LTV): How much is each member worth?

> *(Dues + Non-Dues Revenue) x Average Tenure = LTV*
>
> > *Example: Assume $100 per year in dues and $50 per year in non-dues revenue: ($100 + $50) x 10 = $1,500 LTV*

Maximum Acquisition Cost (MAC): What is the maximum amount that you could, in theory, spend to get a member?

> *((Dues + Non-Dues Revenue) - (Incremental Servicing Costs + Costs of Goods Sold)) x Avg. Tenure = MAC*
>
> > *Example: Assume Incremental Servicing Costs = $20 and Cost of Goods Sold = $25: (($100 + $50) - ($20 + $25)) x 10 = $1,050 MAC*

Rossell says coming up with these formulas can apply to every organization with members. "I look at using this type of analysis in the same way as a doctor taking your basic readings in a physical exam. The only case where there would not be a benefit in knowing your renewal rate, average tenure, lifetime value or steady state is if you are afraid to find out the answer. The purpose of knowing these numbers is to help understand the current membership vital signs for an organization and help them adapt and plan for a different future, if that is what is desired," he says.

Using these formulas can help an organization make better informed marketing decisions, but Rossell says to keep in mind these tools are designed to analyze your current membership situation. "Averages can be deceiving. There may be certain segments within a membership that have a much lower or higher renewal rate. Some segments of a membership might have a much higher or lower lifetime value. So it is important to understand that averages for an entire organization tell an important story, but looking at how individual segments of a membership perform may also be an important thing to analyze," he adds.

Source: Tony Rossell, Senior Vice President, Marketing General, Incorporated, Alexandria, VA. E-Mail: Tony@marketinggeneral.com

Yearly Plan Should Address Key Categories

Whenever you create your yearly operational plan, complete with goals, quantifiable objectives, action plans and a calendar of what needs to happen when, be sure that it addresses key categories.

Those categories may include but not be limited to:

- ❏ New members
- ❏ Retention strategies
- ❏ Member benefits
- ❏ Dues structure
- ❏ Website features

- ❏ Returning members
- ❏ Membership categories
- ❏ Volunteer involvement
- ❏ Fundraising strategies
- ❏ Special events

- ❏ Board relations
- ❏ Member publications
- ❏ Affinity programs
- ❏ Annual conference
- ❏ Member events
- ❏ Membership recognition, awards
- ❏ Recruitment campaigns
- ❏ Member networking opportunities
- ❏ Membership communications
- ❏ Member chapters, chapter relations

- ❏ Member policies, procedures
- ❏ Renewal rates/procedures
- ❏ Legislative programming
- ❏ Members-only programming
- ❏ Recruitment campaigns

Is a Membership Audit Part of Your Strategic Planning Process?

If you are entering into a strategic planning process and you haven't considered a membership audit, maybe you should. President and CEO Dana Hines, Membership Consultants (St. Louis, MO), says by pairing the two you get information about what is going right and what needs to be addressed, and you get a step-by-step plan that charts the path to membership growth and success in the future.

"An audit analyzes what an organization has been doing to acquire, renew and service their members. It looks at the organization's operations to make sure they are operating under best practices and efficiencies, and compares the organization's results to benchmarks within the membership industry, in the niche market they operate within," says Hines.

She says the membership director or manager at an organization is generally responsible for overseeing the audit within an organization, since it will be his or her job to implement the recommendations generated by the audit process.

Audits usually take about 60 to 90 days, says Hines. Clients are asked for a variety of statistics and reports on the past few years of their program. After the data is analyzed, an on-site audit meeting with the client is scheduled to gather any additional information that is needed.

The information is used to write a complete analysis of the membership program and what needs to be addressed going forward. Then, the client receives a report complete with recommendations, an action plan and projections of where the organization could be if the plan is followed, going out three to five years.

In order for an audit to be truly effective, Hines says the

Make the Right Choice In a Membership Auditing Firm

Thinking about looking for someone to undertake a membership audit for your organization?

President and CEO Dana Hines, Membership Consultants (St. Louis, MO) shares a few key points to remember in choosing the right firm to perform your audit:

- Have a good understanding of what you want to get out of the process.
- Talk to people who have used a firm's services.
- Ask for a sample report, so you can see what the end project looks like.
- Check references to see how the consultant performed and how the organizations benefitted from the process.

client needs to be able to provide accurate reports and results of past efforts, be able to present an accurate picture of their biggest challenges and have a top-down commitment to follow the recommendations, including investing in the program in order to grow and succeed. "If they take advantage of the audit and plan, they will be at a different spot five years down the road, with new opportunities and challenges."

Hines recommends that organizations complete a membership audit once every five to seven years.

Source: Dana S. Hines, CFRE, President & CEO, Membership Consultants, St. Louis, MO.
E-mail: dana@membership-consultants.com

Membership Audit Boosts Membership

If membership has hit a plateau, is declining, or if a difficult transition is coming, a membership audit could help your organization.

Facing a 24-month closure due to renovations, Happy Hollow Park and Zoo (San Jose, CA) hired a consultant to perform an audit to strategically guide them through the closure. The following describes the audit process through the eyes of Dana Hines, president and CEO of Membership Consultants (St. Louis, MO), and Danielle Bone-Hayslett, membership director of Happy Hollow.

The Consultant

The first step in the membership audit process is data collection, says Hines. "We learn everything about the organization for the past three years: membership totals, new members, how members were acquired, renewal rates, revenue and other statistics. Then an on-site visit is conducted to get the story behind the numbers. Challenges and opportunities are identified, and specific recommendations are made that tie into the organization's strategic plan."

She says the three-month audit process (which typically costs between $15,000 and $25,000) helps organizations move away from hunch-based responses to membership challenges. "With the audit, an organization gets a data driven, researched, specific plan based on a reliable process. This ensures the right steps are taken to grow membership."

The Client

Bone-Hayslett says her organization was drawn to a membership audit, because they wanted professional guidance in developing a strategic plan to help carry their membership through an extensive closure. She adds that, "We also wanted to capitalize on the opportunity of a grand re-opening for the facility."

The result of the audit was a two-year bridge membership program that generated revenue through the closure. "We maintained a member base of 8,000 households for a facility that wasn't even open!" Bone-Hayslett says. "Our grand re-opening exceeded all projections. We reached the highest number of memberships our facility has ever had, jumping from 8,000 member households to over 25,000!"

For other organizations considering an audit, Bone-Hayslett recommends preparing statistical information in advance. "Start tracking and running reports. Share information on the various membership efforts your organization has executed over the years. And think about the future goals you would like to meet for your membership program."

Sources: Danielle Bone-Hayslett, Membership Director, Happy Hollow Park & Zoo, San Jose, CA.
E-mail: Danielle.Hayslett@sanjoseca.gov
Dana Hines, President and CEO, Membership Consultants, St. Louis, MO. E-mail: dana@membership-consultants.com

The Operational Plan: How to Create a Yearlong Membership Plan

ANALYZE EXISTING MEMBER CATEGORIES: BENEFITS & DUES STRUCTURE

Another important evaluation procedure includes analyzing your current member categories, which includes your dues structure and the accompanying benefits that members receive for each category. You should study member categories both collectively and individually. How well do they all mesh? Does the next higher member category offer compelling reasons to move up to that level? Do the dues for each member category fit the dues assigned to it?

Make Time to Evaluate Membership Categories

Tiered membership categories help identify top fundraising and leadership prospects but need to be reviewed periodically, says Dana Hines, president and CEO, Membership Consultants (St. Louis, MO).

Here, Hines discusses keys to building an effective membership strategy.

How often should organizations review a membership structure?

"To simply keep up with inflation, we recommend adjusting dues every three years. This reflects the economic environment and avoids the kind of drastic rate increases that alienate members."

What should go into a review of membership categories?

"We advise a cost-benefit analysis of all categories and benefits, with particular attention given to the perceived value of benefits versus the costs to actually deliver them.

"Our rule of thumb is that any membership should yield around 50 percent profit. In a $100 membership, for example, the cost of all benefits and the costs of servicing that membership should total no more than around $50."

How many membership levels should there be? And how large?

"Categories should roughly double at every level: $75, $100, $250, $500, $1,000 is a common progression. We also recommend listing all levels on every piece of literature. Some organizations think that only lower categories should be included, but first-time members do join at upper levels, and you don't want to needlessly squander that support."

Are any membership problems especially common?

"Many organizations, particularly those with membership programs built by a board of directors or advisory committee, have far too many membership categories. Streamlining can be difficult, but if people face too many options, they sometimes don't act at all. Better in the long run to lump some things together and create a system that is approachable and understandable."

What should organizations watch out for when restructuring membership categories or benefits?

"Steer away from any benefits that could create ill will. Parking privileges are a favorite benefit of visitorship organizations, but if you have more priority members than parking spots available, you're asking for trouble. It's just not worth it in the long run."

Source: Dana Hines, President and CEO, Membership Consultants, St. Louis, MO.
E-mail: Dana@membership-consultants.com

Don't Shy Away From High-dollar Amounts

A major barrier to membership-based fundraising success is lack of boldness, says Dana Hines, president and CEO, Membership Consultants (St. Louis, MO).

"Financially comfortable board members often underestimate the resources available in communities, and therefore, push for extremely affordable packages."

Organizations need to know and reflect the demographics of their patrons, but they need not undersell themselves, Hines says. "A lot of times there is simply more money out there than people think."

Expand Online Member Benefits

How often do you evaluate the member benefits you offer?

Increasing numbers of organizations are offering online member perks as part of their total benefits program. Here's a small sampling of online benefits to consider:

✓ Screensavers — Provide access to several different screensavers with images related to your organization.
✓ Education, training, certification opportunities — Make e-learning available.
✓ Online store — Offer gift items at a member discount that can only be purchased online.
✓ E-mail address — Offer a members-only e-mail alias.
✓ Audio features — Give members-only audio tours or special podcasts of interest.
✓ Access to online publications — Provide members exclusive insider news and opinions.
✓ Links to members' sites — Allow website visitors to connect to members' professional or personal websites.
✓ Networking — Allow members to network with one another via a member directory, bulletin boards, listservs, chatrooms and more.
✓ Job opportunities — Provide members the opportunity to list job openings and search job openings via your website.

ANALYZE EXISTING MEMBER CATEGORIES: BENEFITS & DUES STRUCTURE

Identify Benefit Categories

As you evaluate the various benefits that attract others to join your organization — and remain members — develop a list of membership benefit categories you can then use as a way to brainstorm new benefits that may fit within the categories you have identified.

Here are examples of membership benefit categories to help you get started:

✓ **Helping members save money** — discounts on products, services, travel, etc.

✓ **Educational opportunities** — CEUs, seminars, conferences.

✓ **Increasing members' visibility** — member profiles in publications and on your website, member-of-the-month programs, listing in your directory and more.

✓ **Connecting members with others** — mixer events, affinity group programming, member-only events, age- or gender-based programs.

✓ **Information** — notifications, printed communications, insider information.

As you consider specific benefits within each category, ask both members and would-be members to share what most appeals to them.

Offer Member Categories for Unique Groups

Expanding membership categories and options can provide your organization a wider prospect base from which to recruit. Along with increasing membership it can add diversity and vitality to your member mix. The following are some unique categories other organizations offer:

- Junior/pre-college
- Nonprofits
- Unemployed professionals
- Retired professionals
- International
- Lifetime members
- E-memberships
- Students
- Bundles — Pay dues for two or three years at a time
- Enthusiast — Nonprofessionals with an interest in the industry
- Military
- Young professionals
- Education institutions
- Government

Make Your Case by Identifying the Real Dollar Value of Benefits

To understand your retention and growth rates, look at your organization through the eyes of a nonmember, says Ed Rigsbee of Rigsbee Enterprises, INc. (Thousand Oaks, CA).

Rigsbee believes that being able to show the return on investment (ROI) of membership dues is critical in selling your membership as a good business decision. And one way to do this, he says, is identifying the real dollar value of each member benefit and service.

How the Process Works:

- Bring a broad sample of members together for a facilitated discussion to analyze every benefit the organization offers.
- Have members determine the dollar value of each benefit. A dollar value should only be assigned to benefits that are limited to members. Legislative advocacy, for example, gets a $0 value because nonmembers benefit from that work. On the other hand, legislative updates get a significant dollar value because only members receive them.
- Challenge members to make the numbers conservative and believable.

- Tally the values to generate a comparison of dues versus value, in real dollars.

Positive Outcomes:

- Reveals where small changes to current benefits can make a big impact.
- Makes recruitment appeals more believable.
- Improves retention for members who participate in the process, and promotes the wise business decision of membership when sent with renewal notices.
- Helps guide strategic planning as leadership learns what members value most.

Utilizing a third-party facilitator to lead the process can help maximize results. It allows members to more candidly share their opinions of benefits without the risk of offending those who deliver organization services. It also allows the facilitator to boldly challenge the members and make sure they arrive at quality, believable figures.

"Showing that membership is a good business decision is essential in this environment where people no longer join just to support the industry," says Rigsbee.

Source: Ed Rigsbee, Rigsbee Enterprises, Inc., Thousand Oaks, CA. E-mail: ed@rigsbee.com

ANALYZE EXISTING MEMBER CATEGORIES: BENEFITS & DUES STRUCTURE

Five Ways to Bolster Your Membership Program

Increased membership results in needed revenue, and a well-managed membership program helps retain members and encourages them to contribute even more.

Although not all of these tips may be applicable to your organization, each can be adapted to fit your particular circumstances:

1. **Develop membership benefits that are meaningful and exhibit pizazz.** Telling someone he/she will receive a monthly newsletter is only important if it's valued by the recipient. Meet with a focus group, conduct a survey or meet one-on-one with members to determine most-valued benefits.

2. **Make a clear distinction between membership levels and accompanying benefits.** If you hope to encourage members (or donors) to increase their level of support, include features that make it enticing to move up to a higher level.

3. **Add elitist features to most desired membership level(s).** If, for instance, a top membership level is $1,000, make benefits at that level the envy of lesser levels.

4. **Offer surprise benefits.** Keeping in step with the principle, Deliver more than you promise, provide periodic benefits in addition to those publicized.

5. **Let nonmembers know what they're missing.** Publicize stories, lists and events to make nonmembers aware of member benefits.

Member Benefits Shouldn't Be One-size-fits-all

It used to be that you became a member of an association or a museum or a chamber and you received a newsletter, some sort of workshop or conference, and advocacy (maybe).

Today's members and would-be members are far more sophisticated about what matters to them. The standard offering of benefits just doesn't cut it.

Rather than sharing a lengthy list of benefits that are the same for everyone, tailor your list of benefits to members' individual wants and desires.

Instead of having one long list of benefits on your website, consider categories of benefits that website visitors can click on for more information:

✓ If you're interested in networking and social experiences ...
✓ If you're seeking professional development and continuing education ...
✓ If you'd like to view a calendar of events geared to members only ...
✓ If you want to explore ways to advance your career....

Beyond how you categorize benefits on your website, take more time up front to discover new members' and would-be members' interests, so you can personalize the package of benefits you offer each.

Explore New Types of Member Benefits

What types of benefits do you currently offer your members? Meet with staff and key members to analyze those benefits and create a list of additional options that may be cost effective and attractive to members.

Member benefits worth exploring:

❑ Free/discounted event admittance
❑ Insurance
❑ Web hosting, design
❑ Availability of mailing lists
❑ Interest group opportunities
❑ Discounts on purchases of supplies, gifts, services and other items
❑ Membership directory
❑ Legal services

❑ Members-only social gatherings or educational opportunities
❑ Special types of recognition
❑ Insider information
❑ Access to restricted website pages
❑ Travel: field trips and tours
❑ Special publications
❑ Reciprocal arrangements with other member organizations
❑ Coupons
❑ Voting privileges
❑ Networking opportunities
❑ Special volunteer opportunities
❑ Consideration for special awards

Keep Testing Membership Products and Services

For dues-paying membership organizations, it's important to keep testing existing products and services and trying new ones. Here are several strategies to help you assess what works and what does not:

- Start a member advisory group to review products/services and identify new ones.

- Have more costly products/services — those you otherwise would not be able to offer — sponsored by a business to reduce your costs. Be in a position to measure members' perceptions of these more expensive items.

- Segment and target your audience with specific products/services based on each group's needs and characteristics.

- Test particular products/services for new members on their first anniversary to encourage a second year of membership.

Embrace the Science of Setting Member Dues

Economic opportunity, market demands and taking advantage of trends are factors that drive dues restructuring, according to Bonnie Massa, President of Massa & Company, Inc. The best process to determine dues amounts requires analyzing competition, history, organizational strengths and data. Massa recommends asking the following questions when setting dues:

Competition — Who else is competing for members in the marketplace? What do they charge for dues? How do the value propositions of other organizations compare to yours? After analyzing these factors, you can determine if dues should be higher or lower than the competition.

History — What benefits does your organization offer now compared to in the past? Have dues amounts moved in an amount consistent with the value offered?

Strengths — What strengths does your organization offer in the eyes of members and the community? What is the value of the benefits members receive?

Data — How many members do you have? At what price level? For how long? What is the demographic of your lifetime members? What percentage of members match the demographic of your lifetime members?

Answering the above questions and analyzing the answers will give your organization a good foundation for setting or restructuring dues. Treating it like a scientific process will help ensure that new dues amounts help achieve organizational goals.

Source: Bonnie Massa, President, Massa & Company, Inc., Chicago, IL. E-mail: bmassa@massainc.com

Create a Menu of Incentive Possibilities

The type of incentives you offer potential members depends on the type of organization you represent and the programs and services you provide. Within those parameters, however, there is no limit to membership incentives you might consider.

Why not create a menu of incentive ideas (such as those shown here) from which to choose, depending on the type of promotion and the group you are targeting?

Membership Incentive Possibilities:

- ☐ Extended (free) membership
- ☐ Reduced conference registration
- ☐ Trinkets, certificates or lapel pins
- ☐ Booklet of useful information
- ☐ Special recognition
- ☐ Entry into a drawing
- ☐ Discounts on purchases
- ☐ Free or discounted tickets to events
- ☐ Free or discounted services
- ☐ Special advertising opportunities
- ☐ Electronic decals or imagery
- ☐ Access to a special section of your organization's website

Develop Annual Calendar For Membership Renewal Mailings

To make your retention efforts as efficient as possible, develop a yearly calendar for sending renewal notices. A quarter-based system works well for many organizations, but an effective schedule may include as few as three to six or more yearly mailings.

When determining your schedule, be sure to balance the number of touches needed to move some members to action against the resources spent on outreach to people who will not respond no matter how many mailings you send.

The Operational Plan: How to Create a Yearlong Membership Plan

BEGIN A COLLECTIVE PLANNING PROCESS

To get ownership of your yearly operational plan, it's important that all stakeholders — staff, board members, key members and others — be fully engaged in shaping your yearly plan. Involve them in the planning process. Share what's expected of them as you collectively evaluate historical data and develop goals and strategies for the upcoming year. What do you most want to accomplish? How will you go about setting measurable goals together? What existing programs might you want to expand, which might you discontinue and what new programs should be launched?

Planning Should Begin With Everyone on the Same Page

Are you about to get a staff planning retreat under way to map out your new fiscal year's goals? A planning retreat — held away from your normal workplace — is a wise move. It facilitates teamwork and establishes focus for every member of the advancement shop.

As you begin your retreat, get every participant thinking strategically by posing a thought-provoking question: "To achieve this year's membership goals, we must be particularly good at the following activities…"

Give everyone a few minutes to think about the question and to jot down the top four or five activities they think will be necessary to achieve the year's goals. Then, go around the group asking each to share only one of his/her activities and explain why it is important. Write out each activity on a flip chart. Keep proceeding around the room taking one activity at a time until everyone has exhausted his or her list. Once each activity has been presented and listed, begin a group discussion with the goal of reaching consensus on the top three important activities for the year.

The completion of this exercise will provide a framework for all subsequent planning.

Annual Retreats Help Staff Design a Team Plan

If you want your staff to be enthused about achieving yearly objectives, they should have a voice in shaping the operational plan. If they own it, they will want its goals realized.

1. **Make staff assignments.** Use a bottom-up approach in preparation for your retreat. Ask every staff member to be responsible for some aspect of planning prior to the retreat and to attend prepared to offer a report and recommendations. Whether you make report assignments based on the job responsibilities of each member or use some other method, this ensures that each staff person has a stake in determining the future direction of your membership efforts and cannot sit back during the retreat and simply make judgments about recommendations being made.

   To be sure everyone is on the right track in preparing their reports and their methods are consistent with one another, you may want to meet individually with staff to go over assignments and then meet again to review their progress.

2. **Select the right retreat location.** If at all possible, select a retreat location away from offices and in a relaxed and quiet environment. In addition to serious planning, retreats serve as a bonding experience — a chance to get to know and appreciate colleagues on another level. This bonding and sharing experience helps to pave the way for team achievement. The ideal length of a retreat is about two days, follow by time to make adjustments to the plan back at the office.

3. **Work from a prepared agenda.** Have a prepared agenda that is distributed to staff in advance. Again, every staff member should have a report to be made at some point during the retreat.

4. **Review the big picture.** During the retreat, schedule times to look at the big picture — what is working well and what needs fixing? There should be time for brainstorming with no limits on what can be said. This big picture discussion will help provide a framework with which to set goals, objectives and strategies.

5. **Begin the process of setting new goals, objectives, strategies, action plans and timetables.** Following a review of your overall membership effort, and how it applies to your organization and mission, you can begin to set new goals along with quantifiable objectives for each goal. This procedure will be linked to your review of each program and whether it should be eliminated, enhanced or left unchanged.

6. **Revisit your plans at various times during and after the retreat.** After you have drafted quantifiable objectives and accompanying strategies that will help to achieve those objectives, move on to something else, but allow time to revisit your plans and make necessary adjustments, since changing one program may have an impact on the others. This revisiting process allows each team member to more fully consider the ramifications of each change being made over the previous year's programs.

   You may even want to consider a follow-up (one-day) retreat a week later to review your operational plan in draft form to determine what changes are appropriate before it is printed in its final form.

A well-organized staff retreat is a critical part of planning your year in advance.

Put Some Thought Into Planning Your Retreat

Scheduling a planning retreat with staff, members and/or board members? The final outcome of any successful retreat is determined, in part, by the planning that goes into it.

Answers to these questions will help you plan a results-oriented retreat:

1. Where will we meet: On-site or at some more relaxed off-site location?

2. How long will the retreat last? A half-day? A full day? Overnight?

3. What will be the primary objective of the retreat? Any secondary objectives?

4. Who will play a role in planning the retreat?

5. Who will be responsible for making presentations or leading discussions?

6. Will a facilitator be required? Should that individual be an insider who is familiar with our organization and its goals or an outsider with professional facilitating experience?

7. What retreat materials will be needed?

8. What outcomes will determine the retreat's success?

9. What types of follow-up will be expected as a result of the retreat?

10. What can be done to help retreat participants think creatively and contribute to their fullest capability?

Pre-retreat Planning Makes For More Productive Retreat

Retreats can provide a very productive way of mapping yearly membership recruitment, retention and programming strategies. They can also result in a debilitating experience if not conducted properly.

To accomplish the most from your planning retreat, hold one or more pre-retreat meetings to see that everyone is on the same page. Begin by meeting individually with staff to review job descriptions and outline what's expected of them for your upcoming planning session. Then assemble as a group and develop a planning agenda that focuses on what you intend to have the retreat accomplish — key membership goals, quantifiable objectives, action plans and key dates.

By developing your retreat agenda as a group, each member's plans and suggestions con be brought together for a much more cohesive planning process.

Planning Retreat Tips

- During a planning retreat, make it your goal to implement at least one idea offered by each participant, resulting in greater buy-in and acceptance of change.

- Collect information from all participants prior to the retreat through interviews, focus groups and surveys. That data then serves as the basis for discussion at the retreat and often saves time.

- Before scheduling a staff retreat, contact representatives from other member organizations — even those unlike your own — to learn more about particular strategies they have successfully used in the past. You may come across a new idea worth exploring during your planning session.

Plug Members Into Annual Planning Efforts

Would you like members to become more engaged in more of your key efforts, even recruiting and retaining more members? Then work to involve them in planning your year and in shaping specific key strategies.

Whether it is by participating in a planning retreat, being a part of a focus group or meeting with you individually, ask for member input that will set the stage for continued involvement as the year progresses.

Members can help plan by:

- Developing a membership recruitment campaign theme and structure.

- Reviewing and commenting on your yearly operational plan.

- Brainstorming new approaches for increasing overall membership.

- Planning a variety of member events.

- Reviewing and commenting on specific member programs (e.g., professional development, affinity groups, volunteer opportunities, members-only benefits and more).

- Brainstorming member benefit opportunities that might most appeal to would-be members.

Combine These Ingredients for Worthwhile Retreats

Retreats can be useful planning or strategizing opportunities for members.

Here are six ways to make your next members' retreat a positive, valuable experience for participants and have them looking eagerly ahead to your next member event:

1. **Plan and organize your retreat thoroughly.** A well-thought-out agenda will demonstrate to participants that you mean business and also respect their time. Stick to your timeline.

2. **Enlist a competent facilitator and/or moderator** to keep attendees enthusiastic and participatory.

3. **Get participants talking early.** The surest way to put everyone to sleep is to lecture to them. Avoid this by seeking audience input and discussing key issues of interest to them.

4. **Treat all ideas and opinions with respect.** Make it clear up front that no idea is a bad idea. Encourage all participants to remember the Golden Rule as they work to plan and resolve issues.

5. **Make the experience motivating.** Help participants become and remain enthused. Incorporate a brief talk from an exciting speaker. Develop goals and objectives participants can support.

6. **Don't forget to make it fun.** Although participants should leave knowing a great deal was accomplished, the experience should also be uplifting. Provide time for socializing, rewarding attendees when appropriate and incorporating strategies that help people to smile.

Ideal Facilitator Characteristics

Looking for a facilitator for that next retreat? Finding someone with the right skills and characteristics to lead a group discussion can be challenging.

As you strive to find the best person for the job, keep these ideal facilitator traits in mind:

- Well-organized and can stick to an agenda without appearing rigid.
- Adept at engendering audience participation.
- Exhibits sensitivity and sincerity.
- Exhibits a good sense of humor and knows when to use it.
- Maintains a high level of enthusiasm.
- Helps to lead participants toward logical conclusions.
- Exhibits negotiating and consensus-building skills.
- Remembers to affirm positive behavior.
- Stays focused on the big picture.

As you visit with potential facilitators, ask for and check with references to discern their capabilities.

When It Makes Sense to Turn to a Membership Consultant

People seek professional assistance — from doctors, counselors, financial planners — in numerous areas of life. Why should organizational life be any different, asks Tony Rossell, senior vice president at Alexandria, VA-based consultancy Marketing General, Incorporated.

Rossell says the following are reasons an organization might do well seeking assistance from outside counsel.

- **Extra hands.** Whether an annual conference, a hectic membership renewal period or a stand-alone project, consultant labor can save money on salaries, recruitment and all manner of benefits, says Rossell.

- **Objectivity.** All leaders can become trapped in inaccurate and unproductive patterns of thought. Consultants can bring a sense of perspective that is unique and very valuable, particularly in controversial or sensitive situations, says Rossell.

- **Proven methodology.** "So often we try to reinvent the wheel when the tools we need have already been perfected and tested," says Rossell, noting that part of the benefit organizations receive from outside counsel is access to years of trial and error.

- **Accountability.** Consultants are particularly effective in establishing accountability, says Rossell. "Being outsiders, consultants can lay out very specific outcomes — generating X amount of memberships for Y amount of dollars — and help organizations really stick to them."

- **Specialized knowledge.** For many organizations, the biggest problem is simply a knowledge gap, says Rossell — a gap the specialized skills of consultants are perfectly positioned to fill.

If money is tight and the decision to seek outside help is difficult, Rossell says most consultants will offer an initial consultation at no cost. "Meet with them, lay out your situation and see where they think they could help," he advises. "If what they have to say makes sense and shows potential for leveraging the organization in ways that staff alone couldn't, then you can think about taking the next step."

Source: Tony Rossell, Senior Vice President, Marketing General, Incorporated, Alexandria, VA. E-mail: Tony@marketinggeneral.com

Encourage Your Members to Bring Forward Ideas

What are you doing to encourage members to step forward with creative ideas that will better your organization and those served by it? Do your members feel comfortable enough to suggest initiating a new program or ways to enhance an existing service? Do they offer ideas for growing your membership or making the membership experience more rewarding?

Use a form similar to this to encourage ideas from members.

It would be wise to encourage and reward ideas from members. Not only might they provide valuable contributions, they will become more engaged in your organization simply by being invited to make suggestions. While some ideas may not get implemented, those that do should get the attention they deserve, as should their originators.

Consider forming a committee made up of both staff and members to review suggestions. If an idea has potential, it progresses to the appropriate management position. If not, the contributor receives a note of appreciation from the committee along with some inexpensive item, such as a pen and notepad set, key chain or other token bearing your organization's logo, for having taken the time to submit an idea.

If an individual's idea gets implemented, he/she receives some form of recognition and internal publicity, plus a special prize — perhaps one that has been donated.

Develop a form similar to the one pictured here and distribute it to your members at least twice yearly. You may be pleasantly surprised at the results.

— NOTEWORTHY IDEAS —

Contributor _____ Date_____

My idea is intended to:

❏ Begin a new program
❏ Generate new revenue
❏ Cut costs
❏ Advance education choices
❏ Recruit new members
❏ Improve chapter programs
❏ Reward/recognize members

❏ Enhance a program/service
❏ Increase revenue
❏ Improve networking opportunities
❏ Improve website features
❏ Retain existing members
❏ Enhance member advocacy
❏ Other_____

Summarize your idea(s):_____

_____

Purpose of idea — What, specifically, would your idea accomplish? _____

_____

How many members/volunteers would be required to successfully implement your idea? _____

How much staff time would be required? _____

What would it cost to fully implement your idea, and what would those costs be? _____

How long would it take before your idea is fully in place? _____

What role(s) are you willing to play to turn this idea into a reality? _____

_____

Additional comments: _____

_____

Please return to Member Relations Department. Thank you.

Use Surveys to Broaden the Reach of Strategic Planning

Times of strategic planning can be a great opportunity to reach out to frontline employees who wouldn't otherwise be involved in the decision-making process. Receptionists might have great insights on services or programs clients would appreciate; drivers or mechanics might have invaluable suggestions on logistics and fulfillment. Moreover, buy-in from these staff members will be key to making the back end of any strategic plan flourish.

Make sure these perspectives are considered by surveying all employees (and possibly volunteers, interns and loyal donors, as well) prior to planning meetings or retreats.

The Operational Plan: How to Create a Yearlong Membership Plan

BEGIN A COLLECTIVE PLANNING PROCESS

Find Alternate Facilitation for Planning Retreats

Outside facilitation can greatly increase the success of a planning retreat, but many consultants are prohibitively expensive. If you are trying to trim your retreat's budget, consider seeking a facilitator at local universities instead.

Many educational institutions will have a professor or two who specialize in areas like consensus-building, mediation, collective decision making or group problem solving. These professionals might well offer their skills at a greatly reduced rate, if not completely free of charge.

Planning Retreat Tips

If you're planning a retreat to discuss and determine membership-related strategies for a new year, make these four points a key part of your discussions:

1. What do you intend to do more often?
2. What will you do less often?
3. What do you want to start doing?
4. What do you want to stop doing?

The direction you take with particular membership strategies will become more clear in the context of answering these four questions.

Keep Retreat Agenda Simple, Focused

While it is only natural to want to get a lot done at your staff retreat, stay focused. Keep the agenda simple, realizing that it is best to decide on one main goal with no more than three discussion topics.

Having a focused agenda will help everyone stay on track, alleviate the pressure of rushing through a jam-packed agenda and give you real solutions to the main issue at hand.

Must-have Ingredients for Strategic Planning

Strategic planning is critical to long-term success, but many organizations confuse it with either annual planning or long-range planning, says Michel Hudson, chief strategist at 501(c)onsulting (Round Rock, TX).

"Strategic planning is a directed effort to shape and guide what an organization is, what it does and why it does it — with a focus on the future," says Hudson. "It uses strategies to define a course of action but remains consciously responsive to changing environmental conditions."

Hudson says effective planning varies in style and approach, but generally incorporates several core ingredients, including:

- A mission statement that defines an organization's purpose, values, constituency and services, in one to three precisely worded sentences.
- A vision statement that provides an image of what success would look like for the organization. "The vision is your dream for the future," says Hudson. "It frames any proposed course of action."
- Pre-planning fact-finding such as conducting internal and external surveys and gathering organizational charts, past strategic plans and collateral materials (e.g., newsletters, brochures).
- Buy-in from all stakeholders, including both internal personnel and external supporters like top donors and supporters. "You can devise a great plan, but if you don't have the support needed to implement it, you've wasted your time," says Hudson.

- An off-site retreat for leadership-level collaboration and planning. "Usually you have a daylong retreat somewhere pleasant and peaceful, because you're going to be addressing difficult issues," says Hudson. To facilitate planning, she says the venue should be comfortable and have plenty of room, places to record brainstorming (white boards, flip charts, etc.), wireless access and a sufficient number of power outlets. She also recommends plenty of funds budgeted for lunch and snacks.
- An outside facilitator to help run the meeting. "A consultant (paid or not) can bring an objective viewpoint to the process, and there is a real skill to facilitation — in being able to accomplish what you need without hurt feelings or political agendas."
- Follow-up undertaken by a designated task manager whose role is to assign strategic objectives to particular people with deadlines, collect data and chart progress.

Finally, Hudson suggests an annual review of the strategic plan. "Enough can happen in a year that you may need to revise your plan. A full planning session should only be necessary every two to three years, though."

Source: Michel Hudson, Chief Strategist, 501(c)onsulting, Round Rock, TX. E-mail: mhudson@501consulting.com

2012 © Stevenson, Inc.   18   www.stevensoninc.com

The Operational Plan: How to Create a Yearlong Membership Plan

Test Brainstorming Methods

Want to explore strategies for growing your membership base? Turn to other staff and members for their input.

Conduct brainstorming exercises to generate ideas that may one day result in useful strategies for attracting and retaining members.

Here are four different methods for brainstorming:

Cubing — Cubing enables you to consider your topic from six different directions; just as a cube is six-sided, your cubing brainstorming will result in six sides or approaches to the topic. Take a sheet of paper, consider your topic, and respond to these six commands.

1. Describe it.
2. Compare it.
3. Associate it.
4. Analyze it.
5. Apply it.
6. Argue for and against it.

Reversal — With this approach, the group examines a goal — say, how to retain more members — and identifies several assumptions about the goal. In this instance, one assumption might be that adding certain member benefits will retain a higher percentage. Once assumptions have been identified, the group tries to disprove each of them, often developing ideas in the process. Trying to disprove assumptions helps to stimulate everyone's thinking.

Mind map — Draw a circle on a white board with spokes emanating in all directions. In the circle, write the topic of the brainstorm — "Events that will attract people to our facility" or "Ways to build chapter involvement." Participants then share ideas related to that topic and the leader writes them down at the ends of the spokes. Ideas build on existing ideas.

Brainwriting — A great method for those who may be less inclined to speak out, each member of the group receives a tablet of paper. Each participant writes down one idea related to the topic at the top of the paper, peels it from the tablet and then places it in the middle of the table. Participants then grab someone else's sheet and can add to it or pass it on and grab another sheet. After everyone has had an opportunity to review and add to others' ideas, the sheets are collected to discuss and form one master idea sheet.

Borrow Ideas From Other Membership Organizations

Watch for other organizations' ideas and procedures you can modify to suit your needs.

Officials with the Lake Forest Open Lands Association (Lake Forest, IL) reformatted membership renewal notices based on a more efficient version used by other land trust organizations, says Holly Meeks, membership and special events.

The simple, less costly one-page invoice replaces a more complex, all encompassing marketing piece, with the change paying off in reduced costs and increased renewals.

"Our renewal rate has gone up substantially as a result of using the new invoice, approximately 30 to 40 percent, and we are saving money," says Meeks. "Because the invoice is such a savings, we are able to do one additional reminder mailing. We find that each of our mailings brings in approximately 30 percent of our renewals."

They mail the invoice in a standard billing envelope, she says, noting: "While I would have thought the bill was too impersonal for an organization always trying to make a personal connection, it turned out to be the factor that indeed got the renewal paid. We're now put directly into the to-be-paid pile rather than the to-be-read-later pile."

Meeks advises paying attention to how other member organizations communicate with members and noting engaging member Web pages or marketing pieces.

"I always keep a file of other organizations membership renewal forms, marketing pieces, annual reports, newsletters, event invitations, etc.," she says. "I peruse them frequently, make notes and often come back to use a part of them."

Source: Holly Meeks, Membership and Special Events, Lake Forest Open Lands Association, Lake Forest, IL. E-mail: hmeeks@lfola.org

This newly designed renewal notice, sent to members of Lake Forest Open Lands Association (Lake Forest, IL) with a standard billing envelope, replaces a more costly, less-effective piece:

Content not available in this edition

Separate Annual and Strategic Planning

When scheduling a session to plan your organization's future, it can be tempting to attack everything at once. That's a mistake, says Michel Hudson, chief strategist at 501(c)onsulting (Round Rock, TX).

"Annual planning should really be done separately from more long-term strategic planning," she says. "The two require completely different kinds of mindset. Strategic planning is focused on thinking outside the box and finding creative, innovative solutions. Annual planning is much more tactical, much more about practical, operational details."

If your organization has trouble finding time to get away for planning, Hudson suggests back-to-back planning sessions on two consecutive days.

Source: Michel Hudson, CFRE, Chief Strategist, 501(c)onsulting, Round Rock, TX. E-mail: mhudson@501consulting.com

'Cloud Thinking' Boosts Collective Brainpower

You've probably heard the phrase "collective brainpower" before. Like most people, especially those looking to improve efficiency, morale and creativity among a nonprofits' membership and staff, you probably think the emphasis is on brainpower — that the ultimate goal is to come up with the biggest and brightest ideas, even if that means creating competition amongst yourselves.

In reality, the key to an organization's success is the collective part. It's about garnering the widest range of input and feedback from the entirety of your organizational chart.

"We all hear about cloud computing, which is about using a multitude of servers from all over the place to achieve one goal," explains Brian D. Olson, founder of Conversation Starters Public Relations (Highlands Ranch, CO). "Organizations have to think the same way, harnessing the collective perspectives of the group. It's 'cloud thinking.'"

It can be difficult, though, to take an organization whose staff, members and volunteers are used to contributing only to their respective niches and start them thinking of their work as collaboration across the organization as a whole.

Here are some moves you can make, recommended by Olson, that are easy to execute, yet signal bold, new ways of collective, cloud thinking:

- **Consider communications campaigns.** TV or radio spots, a new slogan, creating a YouTube channel for your nonprofit — these are no longer something to be dumped on the desk of the development director, says Olson. Media and messaging should be embraced organization-wide and in all parts of the process: brainstorming, feedback, final decisions and helping to get the word out.

- **Bring guests to each and every board meeting.** Olson, who serves on the board of directors at a major nonprofit in the Denver area, says, "I've encouraged the leadership of the nonprofit itself to ask a staff member — someone whose role falls below the level of director — to come and meet us and tell us what he or she does at each board meeting." The same can easily be done with volunteers and members, too.

- **Take board members outside the board room.** Olson and his fellow board members are also required to take part in share-the-load days to fully understand what goes into meeting the needs of the nonprofit. Remember, everyone at your nonprofit has needs, not just the constituents you serve, he says.

Everyone involved with your nonprofit can and should be a brand ambassador. That means that wherever your nonprofit has a presence — both in real life at special events and online on social media sites such as Facebook and Twitter — all employees, volunteers, members and clients should feel that their voices are a part of the mix. Says Olson, "Put them to work."

Source: Brian D. Olson, Founder, Conversation Starters Public Relations, Highlands Ranch, CO. E-mail: brian.olson@ starttheconversations.com

Cultivating Brand Ambassadors

Even corporate America is starting to tap into their existing workforce to help get branding and messages out. Here are some real-life examples of ways you can bring out the ambassadors in your employees, membership, volunteers and other staff:

- Overstock.com and Pizza Hut are just two companies whose ads feature their employees.

- Kraft uses its own employees as one, big focus group, determining the names of certain products, getting feedback on packaging and ad copy, etc.

- Southwest Airlines maintains a blog called Nuts About Southwest that 30-some employees contribute to with frequent blog posts.

- A Coca-Cola brand ambassador program tailored specifically to college students allows the company to garner attention among a young demographic. The students who take on the ambassadorship roles get the benefit of putting real-life marketing experience on their résumés.

The Operational Plan: How to Create a Yearlong Membership Plan

GOAL-SETTING PROCEDURES

It's important that everyone involved play a role in setting challenging but realistic goals based on historical data and future needs. In the end, your operational plan should include lofty goals, quantifiable objectives that will make those goals a reality, action plans that support each of your quantifiable objectives, and a comprehensive yearlong calendar that deliniates the who does what when to tie the details of your plans together.

The Science of Setting Membership Goals

The science of setting membership goals is as much about analyzing internal strengths and weaknesses as it is about reviewing external factors. For the leadership team at the Greater Oklahoma City Chamber (Oklahoma City, OK) the planning process starts with an honest assessment of where the organization is, compared to where they want it to be. Vice President of Membership Lisa Boevers explains their approach:

"When we claim to represent the business industry, we want to speak truthfully. A wide spectrum of companies make up the business community in Oklahoma City and our membership should reflect that diversity. Therefore, when setting goals, we first look at the composition of our member categories. This involves identifying the number of members we have in each category and comparing that to the entire business sector. This reveals both areas of strength as well as gaps we need to fill to better represent the industry. It is important to build on strengths and pursue more members in those categories. With gaps, they often happen simply because a certain type of member wasn't asked to join. This demonstrates why analyzing internal strengths and weaknesses is so important. Sometimes members haven't joined because they weren't asked."

Second, the chamber determines where it is making an impact and who benefits from its activities. The OKC chamber focuses on advocacy and policy, community development, education and workforce issues, and also functions as the local convention and visitors bureau. "These areas of focus make it easier to identify who benefits most from the chamber, and makes it clear to whom membership is most attractive, guiding our outreach strategy and goals" says Boevers.

Finally, in the planning process the chamber determines how to best use volunteers. According to Boevers, "It is important to have volunteers who represent the diversity of the business sector in order to attract a wide range of members. We make it easy for volunteers to recruit by encouraging them to speak about the chamber to the companies they work with or would like to work with on a daily basis."

To summarize, the science of setting membership goals involves analysis of strengths and weaknesses, current composition of member categories, areas of impact and who benefits most, and volunteer involvement. It is also helpful to look at the marketplace and capitalize on trends impacting the industry. This allows an organization to shape its messaging to have the greatest effect. Considering these elements as you plan for the future will position your organization for success.

Source: Lisa Boevers, Vice President of Membership, Oklahoma City Chamber of Commerce, Oklahoma City, OK.
E-mail: lboevers@okcchamber.com

Help Members Realize Challenging, Achievable Goals

As you know, people are motivated for different reasons. Nevertheless, most individuals are gratified when they make achievements. That's why it makes sense to look at every member-related program you have and determine what can be done to make them more goal-oriented.

As you examine each program, keep these achievement principles in mind:

- Goals should be challenging but realistic.
- In addition to an overall goal, include intermediate goals along the way.
- Remember to include appropriate incentives and/or celebrations with corresponding achievements.

- Identify a variety of achievement goal types — those for individuals as well as groups. This helps everyone have an opportunity to accomplish something.
- Allow members input in determining challenging yet achievable goals.
- Once goals have been set, be sure to monitor progress through regular meetings, updates in correspondence and other ways.

People enjoy winning causes, so do all you can to help them win along the way.

What Are Your Quantifiable Objectives?

So many times we wander from day to day reacting to those circumstances that come before us. A week goes by and we are amazed at how little we were able to accomplish.

To reach various forms of achievement with membership programs, it's important to continue to set quantifiable objectives. What can be measured can be accomplished. Want some examples? Try any of these:

- To increase the number of dues-paying members by 17 percent this fiscal year.
- To retain 95 percent of our total members.
- To increase volunteer involvement (five service hours or more) by seven percent in the approaching fiscal year.
- To partner with six corporations — with no fewer than 200 employees — on a project that is mutually beneficial.
- To build membership in our Young Professionals program by no less than six percent in the next fiscal year.

Specific objectives such as these help to focus efforts on projects that matter most. They also offer a level of protection from those who would attempt to divert attention to less important matters.

Set Quantifiable Goals for Member Visits

Although the member organization you represent, along with its total number of members, might be well served by more inexpensive forms of communication, it may be wise to also set a yearly goal for face-to-face member visits.

There's clearly no better way to get to know your members than through one-on-one visits. Those face-to-face encounters allow you to identify what about their memberships matter most to them. The visits also send a clear message that you value each member and want his/her experience with your organization to be fulfilling. And finally, that level of personal contact helps to increase member involvement in your organization.

If member contact makes sense for your organization, make it a priority. Set yearly objectives that are quantifiable, such as: Make 250 face-to-face contacts this fiscal year — average five contacts per week for 50 weeks.

Following each visit, complete a call report that: a) lists the primary objective of your call (e.g., member cultivation, invitation to volunteers), b) summarizes key points of what was discussed and c) lists any follow up actions that should be taken as a result of the visit.

Break Lofty Goals Into Achievable Parts

It's one thing to be told, "You need to increase membership by 12 percent this year." It's quite another to make that happen.

Lofty goals can be debilitating if you let them overwhelm you. That's why it's critical for you to break goals down into achievable and sequential steps.

How you break those goals down is equally important. Get rid of your should goals and focus on what makes achieving them more energizing for you personally.

Beyond goal setting and creating a time line in which to achieve those goals, split your overall time frame into months, weeks and even days. Ask yourself, "What will I need to accomplish on a monthly basis, on a weekly basis and each day?"

When it gets down to your daily to-do list, it's a matter of prioritizing what three to five things you need to accomplish that day, since that's all most people can handle with thoroughness and competence.

Don't let time wasters distract you. As you progress through each week, be accountable, not only to your supervisor, but to yourself. Did you meet that week's objectives? Where did you fall short and why? What behaviors will you change to make up for it?

Create a personal plan for achieving your goals by breaking them down into bite-sized pieces, prioritizing them, sequencing them and tackling them with enthusiasm.

Personal Goal: Recruit 175 New Members in 2012

To make that happen:

✓ Extend membership invitations — through direct mail, personal phone calls, e-mail, public events — to no less than 1,050 would-be members throughout the year (6:1 ratio for acquiring new members).

✓ Make face-to-face calls on 200 would-be members (two contacts per person): 400 total contacts (33 contacts per month or 8.3 contacts per week or 1.65 contacts per day).

Set Face-to-face Recruitment Goals

When it comes to recruiting new members, nothing is more effective than a personal call. So if increasing your member numbers is important, make it a priority to set personal call goals for yourself and other key staff, board members and/or volunteers.

Examples of quantifiable objectives might include:

✓ To meet with no less than five new member prospects on a weekly basis or 20 new member prospects on a monthly basis.

✓ To host no less than four events each year geared toward new member prospects.

✓ To enlist, train and manage a group of no less than five volunteers whose primary goal is to call on and enlist a minimum of 20 members throughout the fiscal year.

✓ To train, manage and direct a board whose goal will be to call on and enlist a minimum of 50 new members throughout the fiscal year.

Get Smart When Setting Goals

■ When setting member-related goals, use the SMART principle: Simple, Measurable, Achievable, Realistic, Time-based.

Member Growth Plan Outlines Goals, Objectives

Does your organization have a plan to address goals and objectives?

To better understand membership goals and objectives, staff with the Interlocking Concrete Pavement Institute (ICPI) of Herndon, VA, developed a two-year strategic membership growth plan.

Designed as a guide for members and staff, the plan outlines implementation and evaluation strategies to reach membership goals and objectives in that time frame.

"Our overall goal is to make ICPI the association members rank as their No. 1 choice," says Jessica Chase, manager of membership and administration and plan developer. "We must clearly communicate the value of membership for current and potential members. The plan was developed to help define current efforts and pursue new approaches to membership development and ultimately reach membership growth goals set by our membership committee."

To achieve the overall goal, they set forth two objectives: retain 89 percent of the association's current membership base and increase membership by 14 percent by 2010.

They identified several strategies to implement the objectives over two years.

Strategies to retain members include converting dropped/resigned members to prospects, developing online new member orientation, providing online membership renewal, developing a communications plan for first-year members and implementing a series of dues collections activities.

Strategies to recruit members include promoting membership at tradeshows, supporting chapter recruitment efforts, developing/revising member prospect kits and offering a discount on new memberships.

A strategic planning committee and a membership committee determined goals and objectives. Within each committee, task groups met between each membership meeting to further define strategies. Members also participated by completing member needs assessment surveys.

With approval from the board, staff implements the tasks within the plan and the 22-member membership committee meets biannually to review, evaluate and adjust the plan as necessary.

Source: Jessica Chase, Manager of Membership and Administration, Interlocking Concrete Pavement Institute, Herndon, VA. E-mail: jchase@icpi.org

Craft a Formal Strategic Membership Plan

Why craft a formal strategic membership plan? To keep from constantly reinventing the wheel, says Dana Hines, president and CEO of Membership Consultants (St. Louis, MO).

"With the amount of turnover in the membership arena, strategic plans provide continuity to an organization's overall membership strategy," Hines says. "Because things are always more likely to come to fruition if they are put in writing, plans also increase organizational commitment to membership growth."

Hines answers questions on this important element of membership growth:

What are some of the benefits gained by crafting a strategic membership plan?
"Boards of directors and even executive directors sometimes have unrealistic expectations about membership growth. Similarly, everybody always says that they want more members, but the willingness to commit the needed resources is often lacking. The process of formulating a membership plan helps both situations by getting everyone on the same page about what is doable, what is not and what level of commitment will be required by different initiatives."

Should organizations have specific numerical goals?
"Absolutely. Quantifiable goals are important for both numbers of new members and dollars of revenue raised. An organization might have a goal to grow membership from 10,000 to 11,000, for example, but also have a goal to increase membership dues by $20,000. Both are important, but of the two, revenue is usually the more critical."

What should the time frame of these goals be?
"Every organization should have annual goals, but realistically reaching these almost always requires monthly goals. And that doesn't mean just dividing the big number by 12. You have to know and account for the seasonality of your membership. If half your new members come from an annual conference, you have to plan for that and adjust other goals accordingly."

How can an organization jumpstart stagnant membership?
"Look at what you haven't been doing lately. If you've been doing a lot of new outreach and not seeing sufficient results, you might want to refocus on your core membership, especially if renewal rates are low or falling. On the other hand, if you have been concentrating on your historic base and not getting a lot of traction, you should certainly consider reaching out to new groups whose interest might be largely untapped so far."

How should organizations go about crafting a membership plan?
"Getting all major stakeholders together is key, but since it is difficult to simultaneously lead and participate, I always suggest that someone other than the membership person facilitate the group. Asking someone from the planning department of a big corporation (board members can often supply contacts) or a professor at a local university business school allows everybody to fully participate in the brainstorming."

Source: Dana Hines, President & CEO, Membership Consultants, St. Louis, MO. E-mail: Dana@membership-consultants.com

Content not available in this edition

The Operational Plan: How to Create a Yearlong Membership Plan

RECRUITMENT AND RETENTION PLANNING

Since membership growth and retention are key to any member organization's health, recruitment and retention strategies should be a hallmark of your operational plan. Exactly what do you intend to do to grow your membership and retain a higher percentage of existing members? What strategies will be new? Which recruitment and retention strategies that were successful in the past will be expanded, and which strategies that were less effective will be dropped?

What's Your Plan for Growing Membership?

Down economy? So what. Don't let external factors impede your efforts to expand membership numbers. Identify growth strategies that will allow you to overcome the odds. Here are examples of membership expansion strategies to include in brainstorming sessions:

- Come up with an appealing one-time event, then make the cost to attend cheaper by purchasing a one-year membership. The Art Institute of Chicago, for instance, once attracted a Monet exhibit that resulted in a drastic increase in membership.

- Offer a six-month membership at a reduced rate and with fewer benefits.

- Kick off a member-recruit-a-member campaign with a goal and special perks for members who produce, or consider making it a contest.

- Offer a one-time multiple year membership at a slightly reduced rate.

- Get a sponsor to underwrite the cost of several new limited-time member benefits you can use to make a special push for joining now.

- Launch a workplace contest. Whoever recruits the most colleagues from his/her place of work wins a prize.

Set Membership Recruitment and Retention Goals

Audubon Nature Institute (New Orleans, LA) is a partnership of 10 museums and parks dedicated to nature through preservation and education activities. The institute serves nearly 30,000 member households, and officials are seeking to not only retain those members, but also grow its membership.

Lani McWilliams, director of member services and ecommerce, shares the nonprofit's goals for growth:

What new things did you do in 2011 to retain or recruit new members?

"We connected with Audubon members more through social media. Our Facebook fan page (www.facebook.com/AudubonZoo) boasts more than 30,000 friends, and our Twitter handle (@AudubonZoo) tweets to more than 3,500 followers and the numbers are growing. We also communicated more frequently via YouTube videos and employee blogs.

"The year 2011 was an exciting time for Audubon Nature Institute as we opened Parakeet Pointe, an interactive feeding exhibit at the Aquarium and Cool Zoo, a wild-and-wet splash zone at the zoo. Extended summer hours from Memorial Weekend through Labor Day provided another new reason to visit the zoo, along with the all-new animatronic dinosaurs displayed during summer as we swapped our initial dinos for a fresh lineup. Each of these initiatives was introduced first to Audubon members through exclusive previews and special offers."

What unique aspects of membership seem to clinch the sale of a membership?

"In our market, Audubon membership is generally a value-based decision. The price point and valuable benefit of free admission to both the zoo and aquarium are what clinch the sale. When speaking with visitors, our sales staff is very familiar with the simple equations we use to illustrate potential savings and are quick to point out what a family of four will pay to visit the zoo and aquarium once, versus year-round as an Audubon member. This is not to say that Audubon members do not see their membership purchase as supporting our mission, because our member surveys and other feedback tell us they do. However, the primary selling point remains a great admission deal to world-class facilities."

How many gift memberships do you sell a year and what tips or suggestions might you share about selling gift memberships?

"Gift memberships currently comprise a very small portion of total sales — less than 3 percent — with the majority of sales occurring fourth quarter as a holiday rush. To promote gift memberships during the holiday season, we run print ads (procured by trading memberships at face value), regularly mention gift membership on Facebook and Twitter, advertise in our monthly e-mail newsletter, include reminders in the members' renewal notices and add homepage messaging to our website at www.AudubonInstitute.org. Our public relations department supports this campaign with a news release and on-air mentions by Audubon media representatives who are regular guests on local morning shows."

*Source: Lani McWilliams, Director of Member Services & E-Commerce, Audubon Nature Institute, New Orleans, LA.
E-mail: lmcwilliams@AudubonInstitute.org*

Build Strong Recruitment Program From Ground Up

Take recruiting efforts back to the basics by retraining your board and other key persons on membership recruiting efforts.

A refresher course with one-on-one and group training will strengthen recruiting skills. Start with a brainstorming session that addresses the following:

☐ **Redeveloping goals.** Hold a strategic planning session to evaluate membership growth opportunities. Define a specific goal and steadfast steps to reach it. Develop a growth strategy that meets income needs to sustain and grow the organization.

☐ **Reviewing your prospect list.** Divide your list of prospects into manageable groups, sending information that caters to each group's interests in order to draw them into your membership. Maintain a current potential member list and send information to them on a regular basis highlighting your member events.

☐ **Refining communication strategies.** Ask current members for testimonials that reflect your membership goals and aspirations to share in communications with potential members and in membership literature. Spotlight value-added benefits.

☐ **Streamlining your membership application process.** Find ways to refine the application process. Develop a process that is welcoming, easy and rewarding.

Develop a Membership Marketing Plan

Creating a formal membership marketing plan is critical to achieving your membership goals, especially in this tough economy, says Ginger Nichols, certified association executive, founder and president of GinCommGroup (Rowlett, TX), which provides consulting services and training to membership associations.

Nichols says a membership marketing plan should not only define your recruitment goals, it should also define your retention ambitions. She recommends including the following sections when creating your membership recruitment and retention plan:

☐ *Key planning assumptions:* An effective membership marketing plan must take into account what is happening in the profession or industry and in the marketplace in which its members and prospective members operate. Making these assumptions explicit provides a benchmark against which to evaluate the continued relevance of the plan. Changes in key assumptions should trigger an examination of the strategies and tactics of the plan.

☐ *Market definition and segmentation:* What is the composition of your market? Analyze demographics of the potential market and compare it to the current universe of members to learn what kinds of members you currently attract and which kinds of prospects you are not reaching. Market segmentation is defined as breaking down the market into smaller, more homogenous groups with similar needs that the organization can successfully satisfy. Target marketing is developing and implementing a specific marketing strategy aimed at a selected segment of the market. This section of the plan should spell out and analyze proposed market segments, determining the fit between the organization's value proposition and its priority market segments.

☐ *Competition:* Once you determine the fit between your organization's capabilities and market needs, consider the other offerings in the marketplace, comparing how your organization's benefits, products and services stack up against the competition.

☐ *Positioning and value proposition:* Positioning is the overall identity the organization projects to differentiate itself from competitors and define its value to members. Positioning should establish a competitive advantage that is reinforced throughout the organization's communications and activities.

☐ *Marketing strategies and tactics:* Nichols defines this section as the nitty-gritty of the plan. Strategies are the broad approaches that will be used; tactics are the specific activities that implement the strategies.

To maximize membership potential, Nichols says, include three broad types of membership strategies: proactive, activity-driven and responsive. Proactive efforts are initiatives specifically aimed at generating new members, such as peer recruitment. Activity-driven approaches link recruitment incentives to other services or programs, such as meeting attendance or program participation. Responsive activities are those designed to close the sale among those who contact the association for membership information.

Include in each strategy an objective, information on how you will track and evaluate your progress and the strategy's cost.

Source: Ginger Nichols, Founder and President, GinCommGroup Consulting & Training for Associations, Rowlett, TX. E-mail: gnichols@gincomm.com

Five Rules of Thumb for Recruiting, Retaining Members

Life is complex and rarely provides the time and resources needed to make the perfect decision. To keep your membership recruitment and retention efforts on track in even less-than-ideal situations, keep these handy rules of thumb in mind:

1. **Retention spending rule:** Keep spending money on retention efforts until those costs exceed the per-person cost of recruiting a new member. This rule can create different retention strategies in different organizations. One retention program might focus on eight to 10 high-touch encounters; another might rely on up to 30 or 40 e-mails, phone calls and mailers.

2. **Growth rate rule:** An average combined growth rate (after drops and adds) of 3 percent is a generally acceptable goal for most member organizations. This rule was widely accepted in strong economic times; today a slower growth rate (or even simply breaking even) might be acceptable to many organizations.

3. **Primary market area rule:** Nearly three-fourths of a location-based organization's membership will generally come from a 10-mile or 20-minute travel-time radius. Prioritize retention and recruitment efforts accordingly.

4. **Psychological price points rule:** Prices ending in sevens or nines often generate more orders and dollars. Use this rule in pricing goods, services and membership packages.

5. **Giveaway pricing rule:** A thank-you gift should cost no more than 10 percent of a fundraiser's suggested donation. Adapt this rule for a wide range of giveaways, including those used in membership drives and campaigns.

Identify, Follow Through on New Ideas

Got a new idea for recruiting or retaining members? Write it down. Think about it. Consider its cost, time requirements and more.

Ideas are worth nothing if you can't remember them and then fail to act on them. To make the most of new ideas:

- **Make it a habit to record ideas as they come to mind.** Carry a digital recorder, a smartphone or even something as simple as an index card to write down ideas.

- **Within several days, take steps to implement the idea.** Develop an action plan. Create a format such as the example shown here and review it at least weekly.

IDEA ACTION PLAN

Date	Idea	Action(s)	Deadline
2/15	monthly open house	review with staff	3/2
2/19	post-phonathon appeal	check costs	3/8

Test New Ways to Recruit Members

Do you find yourself falling back on the same old ways of recruiting new members?

If those old ways are working, keep following them. But continue to constantly explore new recruitment strategies, as well.

Develop a menu of new recruitment strategies you can test throughout the year. Some of those strategies might include, but not be limited to:

- Get the membership processing fee waived for new members who join at your annual meeting or conference.
- Establish rewards at the state level for member chapters or for individuals who recruit the most new members.
- Partner with your area's largest businesses to launch a membership campaign for their employees.
- Link membership to CEU programs and opportunities.
- Include the cost of membership with the fees that nonmembers pay at key meetings or conferences.
- Explore new ways of bringing visitors to and involving them in your website.
- Set up a competition and rewards program for any of your employees who recruit new members.
- Offer special premiums to motivate would-be members to join.
- Offer alternatives (e.g., a monthly payment plan) to make membership more affordable.
- Ask higher-ups (your CEO, board members) to personally contact new member prospects.
- Hold a random raffle that includes anyone who joins during a designated period.
- Conduct a phonathon to directly contact prospective members.
- Examine ways to use your newsletter and other print and e-communications as recruitment tools.

Explosive Growth: From 400 to 10,000 Members in Two Years

The Barnes Foundation (Merion, PA) is a cultural organization that houses 19th and 20th century French paintings. With a new building opening in Philadelphia in the spring of 2012, the organization embarked upon a membership campaign that produced astonishing results. Aidan Vega, membership manager, explains how the foundation grew from 400 to 10,000 members in two years.

Points of Contact — "It sounds simple, but we made a concentrated effort to ask people to join. When people called in advance to reserve tickets for an exhibit, we trained our staff to ask callers to become members. Identifying points of contact with prospects and then asking them to join made an impact."

Direct Mail — "The greatest number of members came from our direct mail campaign. Initially we sent 60,000 pieces. This drove instant results. An added benefit of direct mail is that our highest renewal group is those that joined as a result of direct mail."

Renewal Program — "Prior to 2009 we didn't have a strong renewal program. Now we reach out to members strategically through a series of five directly mailed letters starting 60 days before expiration until two months after. Also, we e-mail members during this time and utilize telemarketing during the month after expiration, if a lot of members haven't renewed."

Source: Aidan Vega, Membership Manager, The Barnes Foundation, Merion, PA. E-mail: avega@barnesfoundation.org

How Vulnerable Are Your Members?

Can you identify those most likely to become lapsed members of your organization? Officials at The Nonprofit Technology Network (Portland, OR) can.

"We've developed a set of criteria that help us predict a current member's satisfaction and likelihood to renew," says Annaliese Hoehling, publications director. NTEN tracks members throughout the year based on five categories of vulnerability:

- **Most Vulnerable** — first-year member who has not attended any programs
- **Vulnerable** — first-year member who has only attended the annual conference
- **Somewhat Vulnerable** — returning member who has not attended any programs
- **Somewhat Likely to Renew** — first-year member who has attended more than one event

- **Most Likely to Renew** — returning member who has attended at least one event

"Our ultimate goal is to move everyone to that most-likely-to-renew category," says Hoehling, "So we build our programming and communications strategies around that ultimate long-standing goal."

This system helps NTEN reach out to vulnerable members with campaigns and incentives. She notes that incentives will only take you so far. "Most membership professionals will tell you that value drives membership. So the most important thing we do for our current, prospective and lapsed members is to continually develop the educational programs and resources that will help them do their jobs."

Source: Annaliese Hoehling, Publications Director, The Nonprofit Technology Network, Portland, OR. E-mail: annaliese@nten.org

Identify Attrition Rate

Do you know your organization's annual member attrition rate — the number (and percentage) of individuals or organizations that were members last year but not this year? By knowing that number, you can formulate specific strategies to make up the difference as you begin each new year.

Marketing Tip

- Explore ways to segment your database, so you can target both members and would-be members based on various criteria: interests, gender, age, location, professional standing and other key criteria.

Rule of Thumb

- Generally speaking, it costs four times the money and time to get a new member as it does to renew one.

Thoughts on Getting Former Members to Rejoin

Are you looking for fresh leads in the search for new members? Sometimes the best place to look is in your organization's history. Reaching out to members that elected not to renew within the past couple of years can provide a warm, captive audience willing to hear about new member benefits.

When targeting dropped members, it is vital to know on what terms they left the organization. Did they not renew because they didn't see value in the association's offerings? Did they have personality conflicts with other members or staff? Was their reason entirely economic? Knowing why they failed to renew their dues will guide your personalized outreach plan.

Four months ago, the National Association of the Remodeling Industry, Minnesota Chapter (NARI MN), located in Minneapolis, MN, started targeting members who dropped at least one year ago. Tim Chase, Member Specialist, explains NARI MN's approach:

Why did you start reaching out to previous members as quality prospects?

"The economy in our industry bounced back, and we had the sense that many members dropped due to economic reasons. Rather than making cold calls to those not familiar with NARI MN, we believed former members represented an easier conversion opportunity."

How do you reconnect?

"We primarily reconnect through phone calls with a simple invitation to rejoin. E-mail has not worked as well, because it is less personal. There is a lot of value in having a conversation to talk about the current state of the member's business and sharing what new benefits the association offers."

On average, how many contacts does it take to get them to rejoin?

"Persistence is important. It often takes four to five attempts before they fill out the application and join the membership community again. Some members have called back months later to rejoin after multiple attempts to reach them."

Which dropped members do you target?

"We target those who dropped within the last two years. If it was over two years, we found that a number of companies were no longer in business. Also, this time frame guarantees the company still has familiarity with the organization, but enough time has passed to improve economically."

How many previously dropped members have rejoined?

"Nine members have rejoined within the past four months. This represents over $5,700 in revenue for the association. As the economy improves in our industry, we expect this strategy will remain effective."

Source: Tim Chase, Member Specialist, National Association of the Remodeling Industry, MN Chapter, Minneapolis, MN. E-mail: tim@narimn.org

Encourage Automatic Renewals With Member Savings

Do you offer your members a yearly automatic renewal option?

If not, consider doing so. You may find it will increase your renewal response rate.

To motivate more members to sign up for automatic renewal, offer a price break for anyone who agrees to the automatic renewal alternative.

This chart gives you a template from which to create a format for your specific organization's member renewal rates.

Membership Level		
Senior/student	$15 ☐	
Individual	$35 ☐	
Family	$50 ☐	$45* ☐
Donor	$125 ☐	$112* ☐
Charter	$250 ☐	$225* ☐
Leader	$500 ☐	$450* ☐
Director	$1,000 ☐	$900* ☐
Automatic Renewal *		

Mine Membership Renewals

Leave no stone unturned when it comes to developing a well-planned renewal procedure. Your membership renewal process should include tasks such as:

- Sending out no less than three personalized renewal notices.
- Offering incentives for early renewals.
- Pre-renewal communications citing the organization's value to the member.
- Personal contact with members whose membership is about to expire.
- Procedures that make renewing easy (e.g., use of credit card).

Seasonal Promotions Encourage Joining, Renewing

To have high recruitment and renewal numbers, it is important to capture the attention of prospective and current members. The Providence Children's Museum offers a new promotion each quarter to increase membership. Kelsey Nagel, communications and marketing assistant, recommends the following to get the most out of promotions:

✓ **Take advantage of seasonal interest.** "Determine what is popular among members during specific seasons. For example, birthday parties are popular with our members during the summer. Anyone who joined or renewed their membership during the second quarter had their name put into a drawing to have a free birthday party hosted at the museum (something members usually pay for). We saw a significant increase in renewal as a result of this promotion," says Nagel.

✓ **Offer items or services of value.** What are the things members highly value? Offer those things occasionally as a promotion to gain added interest.

✓ **Train staff and use points of contact.** During the time period of the promotion, make sure all staff are trained to mention the offer when they interact with current and prospective members. Also, create urgency by mentioning the offer in e-newsletters, social media and other points of contact where members get information about your organization.

Source: Kelsey Nagel, Communications & Marketing Assistant, Providence Children's Museum, Providence, RI.
E-mail: nagel@childrenmuseum.org

The Operational Plan: How to Create a Yearlong Membership Plan

INCLUDE CHAPTER DEVELOPMENT IN YOUR PLANS

Many member organizations have active member chapters covering a wide georgraphic area. If chapters are an important part of your organization, it's important to involve chapter leaders in shaping your operational plan and together, develop a yearlong scheme that identifies a plan of action for all chapters to grow and better serve members. Even if chapters develop strategies that best suit their circumstances, involving chapter leadership in your planning will help to ensure that what matters to them is in line with your key goals.

Solid Steps to Get New Chapters off the Ground

Widening a network of local chapters can spread influence and increase operating funds, but opening new chapters takes planning and organization.

Staff and supporters at the ThinkFirst National Injury Prevention Foundation (Warrenville, IL), an organization consistently increasing its chapters by about 10 percent a year, knows this well.

"We try to support our new chapters in as many ways as we can," says Debby Gerhardstein, executive director.

This support includes a comprehensive resource packet for new chapters and a willingness to answer numerous phone calls and e-mails, but it doesn't stop there. The foundation also includes a one-day training as part of its certification process. This training is currently given in-person, but the foundation plans to introduce webinar conferencing for remote chapters next year.

Membership is further strengthened by a national conference that draws some 60 percent of local chapters. In addition to providing opportunities for professional networking, it offers training in areas like budgeting and fundraising that many chapters find challenging.

Another important element, says Gerhardstein, is the foundation's system of state chapters. Local chapter directors may apply to the foundation to serve as a state chapter director. These state directors act as a liaison between local chapters and the national foundation, oversee all chapter activity in their state, work to recruit new chapters and identify program needs. They also provide a first line of support and resources for newly formed chapters.

"It's the people in the local chapters who actually implement our programs in their communities and schools, and it is our job to do whatever we can for them," says Gerhardstein. "We strive to provide them with the information and materials they need to be as effective as possible."

Source: Debby Gerhardstein, Executive Director, ThinkFirst National Injury Prevention Foundation, Warrenville, IL.
E-mail: Dbg@thinkfirst.org

Six Steps for Starting a Successful New Chapter

The ThinkFirst National Injury Prevention Foundation (Warrenville, IL) offers six steps to get new chapters up and running.

1. **Identify resources:** "Begin with identifying . . . both in-kind contributions (office space, use of phones, fax, copier, office staff, etc.) and financial sources (foundations, grants, salary, donations, etc.). List these two sources in detail. In-kind contributions are a critical factor in securing any funding that requires matching costs."

2. **Develop a business plan:** "This planning stage requires thorough analysis of where the program is now, where it plans to go in the future, and how it is going to get there."

3. **Develop a budget:** "Based on the strategies developed in the planning process, attach costs to each strategy and build an operational budget that includes short-term (one year) and long-term (3 or more years) plans/steps."

4. **Find the funds:** "Write grants to support your strategies. Get organizations to donate in-kind services. Hold fundraising events. Secure corporate sponsorship."

5. **Implement the plan:** "Now that you have a plan, get going! But make sure that you keep tabs on what you're doing and how much it's actually costing. You'll need this information for quarterly reports, newsletters and evaluating your strategies."

6. **Evaluate your accomplishments:** "Did you accomplish what you set out to do? Where did you exceed and where did you fall short? Do you need to adjust any of your strategies based on reality? What did your customers think of your product? How can you improve what you are doing?"

Strengthen Chapter Communications With Social Media

Social media tools are another option for strengthening chapter communications and building a sense of community. The American Library Association (Chicago, IL) uses Facebook and Twitter to reach staff and the individual members of its chapters. The association also uses these social media platforms to set an example for chapters, follow what the chapters are doing and learn from how they communicate to their members.

Facebook is used to provide links to external resources and news stories that are helpful to libraries. The association also uses it to connect chapters to educational offerings, webinars, research and articles produced by the American Library Association (ALA). On average there is one post a week to the Facebook page. According to Program Officer Don Wood, "It serves as another way to support chapters with practical information that can help them operate successfully."

ALA takes a slightly different approach to chapter communications with Twitter. Along with links to resources and content, it posts information about advocacy. As legislation is being considered that impacts libraries or their users, it is posted on Twitter. ALA includes tweets about what the bill is, the stance of the organization and how chapters can support the position. Twitter is an effective platform for advocacy, because it is easy for an organization's members to share information with their followers by retweeting. This can rapidly spread the message.

"We enjoy using social media, because it increases the interactivity we have with chapters. The best results come from providing targeted content that they are interested in and that meets their needs," said Wood.

Source: Don Wood, Program Officer, Chapter Relations Office, American Library Association, Chicago, IL. E-mail: dwood@ala.org

Assistance Helps New Chapters' Formation, Development

Forming new chapters can be key to the growth of any member organization. "We strongly encourage the formation of new chapters. Without new chapters and new members, our association would not survive," says Kelli Romero, membership director with the Grant Professionals Association (GPA) of Kansas City, KS, an organization which has formed 50 chapters since 2003.

She explains that GPA officials actively recruit individuals willing to form new chapters. Once a new chapter is formed, officials at the GPA's national offices assist in any way they can, Romero says. "We send out e-blasts to promote the chapter; we handle all membership dues; we help recruit and retain members for the chapter; and we provide them with chapter toolkits."

The GPA also gives each chapter two Web pages on the GPA website. One page is public, the other is private. On the public page the chapter can post things like leadership e-mail addresses, event calendars and other information for the public. The private page is for chapter members only and contains the leadership roster, meeting minutes, documents, etc.

The GPA national office also provides financial assistance in the form of an annual $1,000 grant for three regional conferences. "Chapters submit to National if they would like to hold a regional conference in the upcoming year. If they are picked, they are awarded with $1,000 to go towards holding a regional conference," Romero says.

Training and information sharing also occurs during quarterly phone conferences between senior leaders and chapter presidents. "We guide them and help them along the way, but we rely on our volunteers at each chapter to hold meetings and help recruit and retain members," Romero says.

A Member-Get-A-Member campaign has also been in place for three years. This campaign encourages each chapter to recruit new members and retain current members. Chapters receive prizes including free conference scholarships, GPA Bucks and a traveling trophy.

Source: Kelli Romero, Membership Director, Grant Professionals Association, Kansas City, KS. E-mail: membership@grantprofessionals.org

Chapter Formation In Six Short Steps

Want to help your supporters establish new chapters of your organization? The Grant Professionals Association gives those interested in forming a new chapter Six Basic Steps to Forming a GPA Chapter:

1. Locate 10 or more interested grant professionals.
2. Contact the GPA national office. Determine that no other chapter exists in your geographic area.
3. Call a meeting of interested/prospective members.
4. Elect officers, approve chapter bylaws, select chapter name, establish meeting schedule.
5. Submit minutes, chapter charter application and other documents to national office for approval.
6. Collect dues and enjoy the benefits of being a GPA chapter.

INCLUDE CHAPTER DEVELOPMENT IN YOUR PLANS

Develop Member Chapters to Strengthen Association

To provide members with local support and increase new member and renewal rates, officials with the Text and Academic Authors Association (TAA) of St. Petersburg, FL, recently introduced a chapter system.

Chapters can be created with a minimum of 15 members, both existing and new. Each chapter must be led by a chapter chair who conducts regular meetings, accounts for how funds are used and reports on chapter activities to TAA headquarters.

When designing a chapter system, determine how it will fit into your organization's infrastructure, says Kim Pawlak, associate executive director. In TAA's case, she says, "We wanted a simple system that would make it easy and attractive for any of our members to start a chapter."

Pawlak shares advice on starting a chapter system:

❑ **Elicit feedback from everyone at your organization** about how a chapter system can be most easily added to your existing infrastructure. Pawlak involved TAA's executive director, office manager, support staff and webmaster in ideas for easily and inexpensively integrating the chapter system. Two simple by products of this feedback have been the color coding of applications so the main office could easily identify each type, and modification of online applications to properly identify new members based on the chapter they join.

❑ **Identify ways that headquarters will provide administrative and financial support.** TAA gives each new chapter a $500 startup grant to purchase a library of materials and hold a member recruitment party. Chapters also receive 20 percent of members' annual dues for ongoing financial support of chapter activities; a chapter-specific website; chapter-specific listserv and customized chapter logo. Local chapters with at least 30 members are offered one free annual workshop of their choice.

❑ **Build in accountability.** TAA provides prospective chapters with a document that outlines responsibilities as a chapter. For example, each chapter must designate a chair who will account for expenses of the group and serve as the central communication point for headquarters and local members.

❑ **Offer exceptional service.** When persons show interest in forming a TAA chapter, they are sent a packet of recruitment materials within two days with membership forms, letterhead and envelopes, membership brochures and a self-addressed envelope for sending completed membership forms. Pawlak follows up within a week of sending the materials.

❑ **Offer exceptional ongoing support.** "As much as I can, I try to go above and beyond what I have promised," says Pawlak. "For example, I've been including a padfolio for chapter chairs in each recruitment package. On the pad of paper inside, I write a personal note thanking them for their interest in starting a TAA chapter and letting them know that they can contact me if they have any questions."

Source: Kim Pawlak, Associate Executive Director, Text and Academic Authors Association, Fountain City, WI. E-mail: Kim.Pawlak@taaonline.net

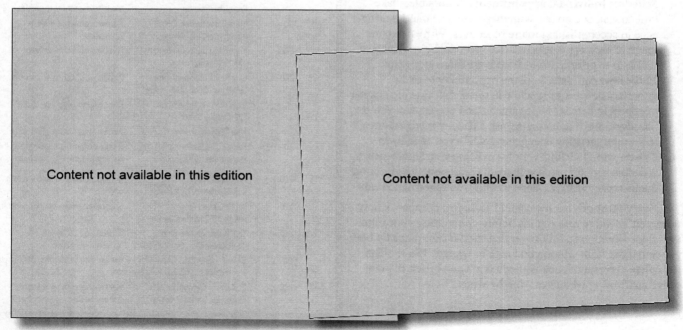

Content not available in this edition

Content not available in this edition

The Operational Plan: How to Create a Yearlong Membership Plan

INCLUDE CHAPTER DEVELOPMENT IN YOUR PLANS

Form New Chapters

If your organization has or supports the development of member chapters, it's important to be proactive, helping individuals form chapters in their communities and regions.
To foster chapter formation:

1. Share success stories (in your communications and publications) of other chapters that have formed.
2. Create a user-friendly template that explains what needs to be done to get a chapter up and running. You might even make a chapter creation kit available online.
3. Take steps to open up communication among chapters to increase the exchange of ideas with one another.
4. Show your ongoing support by scheduling regular trips for chapters to meet with their officers and most active members. Review their accomplishments, discuss future plans and explore what your office can do to more fully support their efforts.

Make the Most of Distant Chapter Visits

Does your position require you to make regular or periodic visits to distant member chapters? If that's the case, prepare thoroughly in advance to be sure you — and those with whom you will be meeting — make the most of your visit.

1. **Schedule multiple chapter visits when possible.** Whether you plan to fly or drive, make the most of your time by contacting multiple chapters in a defined region.
2. **Pal the meeting.** Work out an agenda in advance to avoid spending time on matters that might detract from more important activities. If necessary, schedule a conference call to cover plans and work out details with those in charge.
3. **Shoot for record attendance.** Whether you're scheduling a meeting, a reception or both, take steps to ensure high attendance. For example, encourage your chapter leadership to assign specific jobs to people as a way to get more persons to attend. And incorporate drawing card appeal into your meeting or event. Inform the group that someone of importance will be on hand, publicize door prizes in advance and share an advance list of those who have indicated they plan to attend. Anything that contributes to excitement and enthusiasm will help increase attendance.
4. **Schedule individual appointments.** If possible, make time to visit one on one with those who can make a difference in accomplishing future objectives. Write down the intent of each appointment before scheduling it. Doing so will help to prioritize which ones are more important.
5. **Make new contacts.** Take the opportunity to make important new contacts while in town. Ask existing chapter members to help set appointments and accompany you on introductions. If appropriate, ask a chapter representative to set up a speaking engagement while you're in town.
6. **Create added visibility.** Enlist existing chapter contacts to schedule appointments with media representatives or bring media representatives along as guests to scheduled events.

Every facet of your trip should include a purpose. Know what you intend to accomplish before committing your time. Pay close attention to follow-up that should take place by both you and those with whom you come in contact. Make a list. Complete correspondence immediately upon return to your office confirming who does what by when.

CHAPTER VISITS SCHEDULE

Destinations:	Greater Cincinnati, OH and Boston, MA
Dates of Trip	July 14 - 17
Flight Information:	7/14 Leave 6:40 a.m. United 436 — Arrive Cincinnati 8:10 a.m.
	7/17 Leave 1:40 p.m. United 811 — Arrive Boston 3:08 p.m.
Lodging Information:	Holiday Inn Cincinnati I-275 North, 3855 Hauck Road, 45241. Ph 513.563.9679.
Rental Car:	Payless — Conf# 20204GH

Date	Time	Group/Individual & Location	Objective
7/14	3:00 p.m.	Downtown Chapter Officers Haskins Law Office, 3000 Liberty	Review chapter plans
	5:00 - 7:30	Downtown Chapter Reception/Program	Meet membership, review plans and involvement opportunities
7/15	7:30 a.m.	Breakfast w/Robert Orsman Ritz-Carlton, 419 Omega	Review approach to Kaylor Foundation
	9:00	Kaylor Foundation w/Orsman 102 Bell Avenue	Present partnership proposal
	12:00 noon	Lunch with Norwood Chapter Lieberman Clinic, 334 1st Ave.	Review plans/accomplishments to date
	2:30 p.,.	Meet with Linda Hamilton 202 Ordway Street	Enlist help to begin new chapter
	4:30	Mike Townsley, Fairfax Ch Pres	Review reception program, setup
	5:30 - 7:30	Fairfax Chapter Reception Harford Inn, 109 Belshire	Meet membership, review plans and involvement opportunities
7/16	10:00 a.m.	Martha Corbett 405 Oak Street, Golf Manor	Introduction and invitation to join
	11:30	Ian Ferguson Hilton, 10 Country Club Dr.	Update and review of noon program
	12:00 noon	Golf Manor Rotary Club 10 Country Club Dr, Golf Manor	Presentation and invitation to become involved
	6:00 p.m.	Dinner w/Elmwood Chptr Officers Hockenberry's, 202 2nd Ave., Elmwood	Review membership recruitment plans
7/17	11:00 a.m.	St. Bernard Chapter Brunch Pickles, 89 5th St., St. Bernard	Meet membership, review plans and involvement opportunities

Offer Engaging Webinars to Assist Chapter Leaders

Webinars have become an efficient way yo reach out to chapters and offering training to members. At the American College of Healthcare Executives (ACHE) of Chicago, IL, webinars have proven to be an effective way to offer assistance to chapter leaders in managing their chapters.

ACHE offers 10 to 12 webinars per year, with most sessions held over the lunch hour. Webinars are presented live and are recorded, allowing a longer shelf life of the content and a broader reach to chapter leaders.

Terra Levin, ACHE's regional director, offers the following tips for working with a conferencing vendor and developing a webinar calendar for members:

- Gather feedback about the challenges facing your chapters, and build your topics around those challenges. If some of your chapters struggle in the board transition process, for example, a webinar covering details about chapter management could fill in some holes for a new board member. Generating topics that relate to a new product or service is another good idea.
- List your entire webinar schedule for the year, and give members the option of registering online.
- Offer a live broadcast of all webinars, but also record each session to reach more members at a later date.
- Try to make the webinar as interactive and conversational as possible. Avoid excessive scripting and use photos of your speakers to personalize the presentation.
- E-mail your panelists with detailed information on how to ensure the audio is high-quality. For example, have speakers use a landline and call in ten minutes prior to the call for a sound check.

Source: Terra L. Levin, Regional Director, American College of Healthcare Executives, Chicago, IL. E-mail: tlevin@ache.org

Form, Nurture a Chapter Relations Committee

Having healthy, well-functioning chapters can significantly bolster an organization's membership and impact. It is essential to support chapters with resources and ensure leadership feels connected to the overall mission established by the parent organization. Forming a chapter relations committee is one way to support and connect with chapters to help them effectively serve their members.

The American Library Association (Chicago, IL) has a chapter relations committee where members appointed by the board of directors perform the following:

- Encourage discussion, activities and programs that support the mutual interests of the American Library Association (ALA) and its chapters.
- Advise on proposals and actions of other ALA units that affect chapters.
- Provide a forum where chapters can share ideas and concerns and identify common needs and goals.
- Communicate chapter needs and goals to ALA, and ALA goals and programs to chapters.
- Periodically formulate and review requirements.
- Encourage and maintain a cooperative and supportive relationship among ALA and the chapters.

Michael Dowling, ALA's director of the Chapter Relations Office explains how the committee performs those tasks. "We have a staff of two that works in tandem with the committee to serve the chapters. Because our membership is widespread, the chapter relations committee only meets in person twice a year. However, there is a conference call every six weeks where members share resources, engage in strategic planning and inform one another of new opportunities. This committee is essential in providing oversight and keeping chapters connected."

To foster good chapter relations it is helpful to give those organizations freedom and autonomy. Make sure the policies and procedures provided to chapters are not too constricting, but instead reduce the learning curve as they serve members with needs unique to their geographic areas and circumstances. A one-size-fits-all approach, though convenient, can harm the satisfaction levels of chapters that feel the parent organization is out of touch. Happy members are productive members. Utilize a chapter relations committee to build mutually beneficial relationships.

Michael Dowling, Director, Chapter Relations Office, American Library Association, Chicago, IL. E-mail: mdowling@ala.org

Use Meetings to Motivate Chapter Leadership

Keeping member chapters vibrant and active can be challenging. That's why meetings involving your chapter leaders should include elements that enthuse and motivate them to accomplish even more than they had imagined.

To inject more enthusiasm/motivation into your meetings:

- Identify individuals' recent accomplishments, giving credit where credit's due.

- Establish between-meetings-goals with accompanying rewards that can add an element of fun and competition.
- Devote part of each meeting to reviewing and applauding team accomplishments.
- Invite your CEO or a board member to accompany you on a chapter visit to offer words of praise to those involved.
- Offer an occasional prize for the most creative idea and other key contributions.

The Operational Plan: How to Create a Yearlong Membership Plan

MEMBER EVENTS, PROJECTS

As you map out your upcoming year, identify key events and projects that support your goals and quantifiable objectives. Evaluate last year's events and projects to determine if they should be changed, expanded or discontinued. By identifying your key events and projects early on, you can include all of the planning details of "who does what when" in your yearlong master calendar.

Set Measurable Event Objectives

As you plan events for an upcoming year, it's important to set quantifiable objectives that will allow you to measure achievements and surpass previous years' accomplishments.

When it comes to event planning, what might you include as quantifiable objectives? Here are some examples to help get your wheels turning:

- To generate $X in special event net income throughout the fiscal year.

- To attract X event attendees throughout the upcoming fiscal year.
- To plan and coordinate X events that attract ttargeted audiences ... (e.g., members from a particular profession, would-be members, young professionals).
- To increase the percentage of first-time event attendees by no less than X percent in the upcoming fiscal year.
- To generate a minimum of $X in sponsorship revenue throughout the fiscal year.

Tips Illustrate Planning Tasks for Member Events and Projects

Here are three tips to keep in mind when planning an event or project for your members:

1. When developing a project timeline, begin with the final (finished) project and work backward. Identify major steps, giving each a deadline. Next, go through the process again, breaking each major step into its respective components and attaching deadlines/dates to

each. This back-step approach helps illustrate all that will need to happen to carry out the project.

2. For checklists, list names of person(s) responsible next to each item.

3. Include follow-up and evaluation as concluding components of any project timeline.

Event Preplanning

When preplanning a new event for your membership organization, make the planning phase go more smoothly by having key information in hand before bringing others into the planning stages.

Follow this preplanning guide to assist you when speaking to staff, volunteers and vendors about your newest event:

- ❑ Date of event
- ❑ Purpose of event
- ❑ Event start and end time

- ❑ Number of people expected to attend
- ❑ Venue preference
- ❑ Event title
- ❑ Potential sponsors/donors
- ❑ Event type (meeting, banquet, special event, etc.)
- ❑ Reason for the event
- ❑ Special equipment needs
- ❑ Preliminary budget

Layer Subsequent Years' Events With New Volunteer Duties

Newly created events evolve one of two ways: 1) After a year or two interest wanes and the event is dropped or, 2) the event builds year after year, into a highly anticipated and well-attended occasion.

The direction an event takes is hugely dependent on the planners' level of enthusiasm for it and the degree to which volunteers become involved in owning it.

Assuming those who implement the event are enthusiastic about its purpose and potential, it's important to continue adding layers of volunteer involvement and ownership year after year, being mindful not to divert attention away from previous years' components.

Not only will increased volunteer involvement generate greater enthusiasm and higher attendance, it also allows new event components to be added — child care, continuing education, tours, a reception, etc. — that were not possible in previous years. Continue the fine-tuning process to maintain enthusiasm.

Event Type:
Annual membership kickoff reception for museum or art center

Year One — 10 Volunteers
- Assist in sending invitations, promoting the reception and serving as hosts.

Year Two — 20 Volunteers
- Send invitations, promote reception and serve as hosts.
- Secure a major sponsor for the opening of a major exhibit.

Year Three — 30 Volunteers
- Send invitations, promote reception and serve as hosts.
- Separate committee charged with encouraging members to bring a prospective member.
- Secure a major sponsor for the opening of a major exhibit.
- Expand invitations to families and have separate hands-on entertainment for children.

The Operational Plan: How to Create a Yearlong Membership Plan

MEMBER RECOGNITION

Member recognition programs and strategies should be included in your yearlong operational plan. What you do to recognize members, along with the ways in which you do that, are key to any long-term retention. Examine the ways in which you recognize your members and decide what changes should be made as you document your yearlong plan.

Are You Making a Sufficient Number of Awards?

There's nothing like a well-deserved award to warm the hearts of those associated with your nonprofit or association.

While it's important to make awards for legitimate reasons, there's no denying they also serve to cultivate relationships in significant ways.

Based on your type of organization and your mission, are there monthly, quarterly or annual awards you could be making to worthy recipients? Have you explored the many possibilities? Some examples of award recipients include:

- Members, board members and/or volunteers
- Chapter leaders
- Individuals (men and/or women)
- Youth
- Senior citizens
- Families
- Minorities

- Persons with special needs
- Other organizations or associations
- Businesses and corporations
- Persons who exemplify your mission

To celebrate your member-based organization and the people who make all you do possible, consider giving awards based on:

- Service to your organization
- Service to the community, region, state or nation
- Years of service
- A good deed
- An act of heroism

Where do awards opportunities exist for your organization? Assemble your awards committee and explore the possibilities.

Thank Members With VIP Programs

Looking for a way to thank certain members for their participation and support? Consider creating a VIP program that provides a select group of members with additional benefits and services.

In February, staff with the Lake Champlain Regional Chamber of Commerce (Burlington, VT) created a VIP program for members who frequently attended their business after-hours networking events.

"We wanted to do something that thanked our regular business after hours attendees and highlighted them to the other members," says Susan B. Fayette, director of member development and benefits.

The VIP program application asks for a $45 one-time fee, basic contact information, credit card information to process the $45 fee to cover program costs and, if the applicant would like a coupon book at a discounted price.

VIP program recipients receive:

✓ A permanent nametag with chamber lanyard to wear at all events.
✓ A $10 discount on the chamber's $60 coupon books.

✓ Walk-in price of $8 per event ticket, a $4 savings per ticket.
✓ Entry in a monthly drawing featuring sponsor-donated prizes such as restaurant gift certificates.
✓ An invitation to the chamber's annual VIP-only luncheon, which is paid for by a sponsor and is free to attend.
✓ Placement of the VIP member's name and company on the VIP page of the chamber's website.
✓ Special check-in at events, which includes the member's nametag waiting for them at the check-in table, regardless of whether they have pre-registered.

As of May, some 20 members had signed on for the VIP program. Fayette says members often ask how they can become part of the VIP program when they see their fellow members receiving the VIP treatment at events. For the most part, the program has become invitation only, with Fayette reaching out to members at the business after hours events to let them know how they can join the program.

Source: Susan B. Fayette, Director of Member Development and Benefits, Lake Champlain Regional Chamber of Commerce, Burlington, VT. E-mail: susanb@vermont.org

Offer Specialty Awards to Exceptional Members

Always be on the lookout for ways to recognize and share member accomplishments.

Staff with the Fox Cities Chamber of Commerce (Appleton, WI) grant specialty awards to members who contribute to the community, says Pamela Hull, vice president-membership services

One such honor is the Athena Award, given annually to an exceptional businesswoman who: 1) has achieved the highest degree of professional excellence, 2) has assisted women in reaching their potential and 3) possesses an impactful body of work.

"The Athena Award honors women business leaders for their exceptional contributions to their company, their industry, their community, their chamber and to the advancement of women in business," Hull says. She adds that the chamber is among the charter group of chambers to host the awards since the program's inception in 1985.

More information about the Athena Award is available at www.athenafoundation.org.

Source: Pamela Hull, Vice President, Membership Servcies Manager, Fox Cities Chamber of Commerce, Appleton, WI. E-mail: phull@foxcitieschamber.com

Honor Member Anniversaries In Numerous Ways

Recognizing members' ongoing commitment and loyalty to your organization is a simple but key component in membership retention.

Officials with the Sioux Falls Area Chamber of Commerce (Sioux Falls, SD) recognize member anniversaries by posting them prominently on the main page of the organization's website (www.siouxfallschamber.com). Selecting the Click Here For Member Anniversaries button takes website visitors to a listing of member milestone anniversaries taking place that month.

Betty Ordal, membership services director, offers the following tips for honoring member anniversaries, based on ways the chamber celebrates these important members:

✓ **Send a personalized letter to arrive near the anniversary date.** The chamber sends a letter signed by the chamber president pointing out the chamber's and the member's accomplishments.

✓ **Offer members a memento to recognize their anniversaries.** At the chamber, members may request a plaque signifying the years they have been members. The plaque depicts a background of the waterfall for which the area is known and is mounted on a cherrywood frame. Ordal says that many members display all anniversary plaques in their businesses or can replace a five-year plaque with a 10-year plaque, for example.

✓ **Personalize gift delivery.** At the chamber, staff hand-deliver anniversary plaques during unannounced visits. Ordal says the surprise acknowledgement is a welcome treat to members and allows chamber staff to become better acquainted with members and member businesses.

✓ **Recognize anniversaries in publications.** Member anniversaries are noted in the chamber newsletter, which is inserted into the local newspaper (30,000 circulation) the first Monday of each month and mailed to 5,000 chamber members.

✓ **Use annual dues payment to recognize anniversaries.** Member anniversaries take place one year from the date of inception at the Sioux Falls Area Chamber, therefore, when annual membership dues are paid, this signifies member anniversary dates, as well. When dues are paid, the chamber membership staff sends an e-mail thanking members for continuing their membership. Ordal says staff members often reply to this e-mail with specific information on the trends of their business.

Source: Betty Ordal, Membership Services Director, Sioux Falls Area Chamber of Commerce, Sioux Falls, SD. E-mail: bordal@siouxfalls.com

> The Web page that celebrates member anniversaries at the Sioux Falls Area Chamber of Commerce (Sioux Falls, SD) includes the lead-in paragraph, below. Member listings feature links to information on each business and its website:
>
> ## April Member Anniversaries
>
> Congratulations to the following members who are celebrating their 25-plus, 20-, 15-,10- and five-year membership anniversaries this month. They are part of a continued commitment to our community through their investment in the Sioux Falls Area Chamber of Commerce. To learn more about Chamber membership, contact 605.336.1620 or sfacc@siouxfalls.com.

The Operational Plan: How to Create a Yearlong Membership Plan

PUT YOUR PLAN INTO WRITTEN FORM

Once the planning has been completed, it needs to be documented as your written guide for the upcoming fiscal year. In addition to the five key components mentioned earlier — goals, quantifiable objectives, strategies, action plans, timetable — you may wish to include job descriptions for each member of your team and committee descriptions for key board members and volunteer groups involved with your membership efforts.

How to Prepare and Draft a Membership Marketing Plan

Membership organizations focus on few things more fervently than acquiring new members. And few things are more central to this than creating an effective membership marketing plan.

Here, Mark Levin, president of the business management consulting agency, BAI Inc. (Columbia, MD) and executive vice president of the Chain Link Fence Manufacturers Institute (Columbia, MD), discusses the ins and outs of this important recruiting tool.

What are the questions that need to be answered before developing a membership marketing plan?

"You need to know where the plan ranks among your association's priorities. If you don't have the full support of staff and volunteer leadership, you shouldn't undertake a plan. You also need to clearly define how you will measure success. Take, for example, a goal of increasing membership by 10 percent. Will you take any members you can get, or do you want to target specific demographics? Is retention important to you, or do you not care how many people you lose as long as the total grows by 10 percent? Differing answers to these questions can lead to sharply differing plans, even though they share the same ultimate goal."

What are some of the key elements of a well-crafted marketing plan?

"The presentation document should include the central objective, measurement criteria, key initiatives, a summary of current ongoing initiatives, concrete membership goals, and, I recommend, at least one new initiative planned for each key area of the plan. The membership department should also have the details of implementation worked out internally, though those won't be shared as widely."

Are there elements of a membership plan that are often overlooked?

"Any plan is based on assumptions — assumptions about what the economy will do, what the industry will do, what the government will do. These assumptions should be made explicit and included in the plan, so that it can be adjusted if those conditions change and evolve."

> *"Any plan is based on assumptions — assumptions about what the economy will do, what the industry will do, what the government will do. These assumptions should be made explicit and included in the plan, so that it can be adjusted if those conditions change and evolve."*

What sort of time frame should a membership marketing plan address?

"Any plan of any significant detail over two years long is difficult to stick to because the membership environment changes so quickly. Anticipating conditions more than two years out is guesswork as much as anything."

Are there mistakes organizations often make in producing a marketing plan?

"Many plans are very weak on prioritization. Everybody can generate numbers and goals, but those goals have to be prioritized to determine the order to expend resources. You have to be able to say which parts of the plan you have to have, and which parts you would only like to have. This tells you what could be cut if needed, because something always has to be cut in the end."

You have a membership marketing plan in hand; what should you do to most effectively implement it?

"You should make sure that you are regularly adjusting it, as the assumptions it was based on change. When people fixate on one number or one approach and fail to take into account changes in the environment, they tend to assume their plan was just wrong from the beginning. But that's often not the case. You might have created the right plan for the right time, but the times changed underneath you."

Source: Mark Levin, President, BAI, Inc. and Executive Vice President, Chain Link Fence Manufacturers Institute, Columbia, MD. E-mail: Mlevin0986@aol.com

Your Printed Plan Should Be Used Throughout the Year

A well thought-out operational plan will break down lofty goals into achievable increments. It allows one to establish challenging but attainable goals.

Keep in mind that an operational plan refers to goals that are to be achieved throughout a given year. A strategic plan, on the other hand, is longer-term and more comprehensive. It becomes your organization's vision for the future.

A yearly operational plan should be linked to your institution's larger strategic plan. The operational plan should address the strategic plan and help make it a reality.

There are five key components to a written operational plan:

- **Goals.** Goals are larger in purpose and often institution-wide, crossing departmental lines. They are an outgrowth of the organization's mission statement and help to define what is envisioned be achieved throughout the course of a year. They tend to be more broad and less quantifiable. Examples of goals might include: to become less dependent on dues revenue, or to provide members with the most advanced, cutting-edge educational opportunities available.

- **Objectives.** Objectives are quantifiable and spell out what will be done to address each goal. It's common to have several quantifiable objectives that address each of the organization's goals. For membership offices, examples of objectives might be: to recruit no less than 75 new members throughout fiscal year 2012-13 or, to generate $250,000 in membership revenue this fiscal year.

- **Strategies.** Strategies represent another step in the planning process. They often represent individual programs that define how a portion of an objective will be achieved. It's common for one objective to include a number of strategies.

- **Action Plans.** As we move into more of the detail of how to address goals and achieve objectives, action plans provide the recipe for each strategy and delineate who is responsible for doing what and when. An action plan could be described as a checklist of what needs to happen. While each strategy will include only one action plan, each action plan will include many step-by-step points.

Sometimes one individual is responsible for managing the entire plan, but many of the staff team

Yearly Plan Needs Focus

Your organization undoubtedly has a written plan identifying the year's objectives, what needs to happen by when and who is responsible. Still, it's important for every team member to agree on what matters most. To accomplish this, create a primary focus that takes precedence over all other objectives. Examples:

- ✓ To increase by 10 percent the number of members in our highest-paying dues category.
- ✓ To increase the number of first-time members by nine percent.
- ✓ To initiate strategies that generate more business community support.
- ✓ To produce and present no less than 12 group membership proposals to area businesses.

are assigned to certain tasks. This form of management allows each staff member to be in charge at various times and for various programs and also encourages everyone to work together, knowing they will each be dependent on one another at some point as they work to achieve common objectives.

- **Timetable.** Once all strategies and accompanying action plans have been determined for the year, those involved can go back through each program to pull out dates of everything from get membership campaign brochure copy to printer to chapter officers meeting to send after-hours reminder e-mail to entire membership.

The completion of this master calendar of what needs to be completed by when serves as the centerpiece of activities throughout the entire year. This annually printed operational plan then becomes a working tool that is referred to and monitored each week throughout the year. Often additional information is included in the document — job descriptions, organizational charts, membership policies, procedures and more.

The existence of an operational plan also allows staff to better evaluate existing programs throughout the year and at year-end. This ongoing evaluation process enables the following year's planning to take place with much greater understanding and ease and helps to build on the successes of the past to achieve even loftier goals.

Action Plans Define Quantifiable Objectives

A yearly operational plan should include goals, quantifiable objectives and action plans that define how and when those objectives will be fulfilled.

Although all three components are important, action plans really spell out the how-to of each strategy and, therefore, should be well thought-out in advance. The generic example shown here illustrates what an action plan might look like.

Be sure to include these four elements in your action plan:

1. **Goals:** More lofty in nature; support the organization's overall strategic plan.
2. **Objectives:** Quantifiable; tie directly to goals.
3. **Action Steps:** Key strategies for how you intend to achieve each objective.
4. **Calendar:** Detailing schedule of who is to do what, by when.

If your organization has used a particular strategy in prior years, it will be easier to document what needs to occur and when. For instance, if you had a 10-day member-recruit-a-member campaign in prior years to help meet your membership recruitment objective, creating a member-recruit-a-member action plan should be relatively easy. It's a matter of putting the steps on paper and fine tuning any changes.

Action Plan: Member-recruit-a-member Campaign

Supports following Objective: To recruit 175 new members in the upcoming fiscal year

Campaign Target: 100-plus new members

Action Steps	Date(s)
Recruit co-chairs	June 20-24
Recruit team captains	July 11-15
Team captain meeting	Aug. 1
Recruit callers	Aug. 8-26
Campaign postcards to print	Aug. 19
Prepare handout materials	Sept. 12-30
Send campaign announcement notices	Sept. 16
Send training session materials	Oct. 3-7
Training sessions	Oct. 9-10, 16-17
Campaign calls	Oct. 9-13; 16-20
Call-back/follow-up session	Oct. 23-25
Volunteer party & awards	Oct. 27

Strategies Define How You Plan to Achieve Objectives

Strategies are fun. They get into just how you plan to achieve quantifiable objectives. Often a strategy may represent a particular program.

As an example, let's identify possible strategies you might have to achieve the following annual membership objective: to recruit 175 new members throughout fiscal year 2012-13.

Examples of possible strategies might include:

✓ Increase the number of face-to-face calls to new prospects by X percent.
✓ Generate X more gift memberships over the previous year.
✓ Develop three targeted direct mail appeals aimed at non-members on our mailing list.
✓ Enlist a volunteer committee to review lists of non-members and make X calls per volunteer per month.
✓ Initiate a contest-driven member-recruit-a-member campaign with no less than 50 participants.
✓ Meet with board members and invite them to each approach three new prospects for membership.
✓ Expand our existing prospective member event, building attendance by X new participants.
✓ Create a new special event with anticipated first-year attendance of X.
✓ Provide presentations to civic groups to generate X new members.

✓ Conduct three direct mail appeal tests aimed at individuals or groups not currently on our mailing list (e.g., a particular ZIP code, those with memberships in a particular organization, those in our area who subscribe to a particular magazine, etc.).

There are any number of strategies you can develop depending on the type of organization you represent, the make-up of your constituency and your organization's past membership history.

Spell Out How You Plan To Increase Gift Revenue

Let's say your organization received 145 new members last year. This year's goal has been set at 175 — a 21 percent increase.

In addition to preparing a written operational plan that spells out how you intend to recruit 175 new members, include a quantitative section that outlines how you intend to recruit 30 more members than the previous year. Overcompensate while planning to allow for any shortfalls.

Detailing what needs to occur to realize an increase of 30 members more than last year will keep everyone keenly aware of those important strategies.

Make Volunteer Involvement a Part of Your Plans

As you prepare an operational plan for your fiscal year, be sure to include a volunteer component to engage members and build loyalty. Volunteers can really allow you to accomplish more if you put ample thought into planning for their involvement. And by delegating tasks to volunteers, you'll have more time available for paid staff to focus on other priorities.

Pencil volunteers into your year plan for any number of tasks, including:

- Making membership calls.
- Reviewing and screening prospect names.
- Making phone calls.
- Calling on members and businesses to say thanks.
- Taking photos, conducting tours and more.
- Helping coordinate member events.
- Serving as ambassadors.
- Assisting with behind-the-scenes duties.
- Staffing informational booths at community events.

Your written operational plan — complete with goals, quantifiable objectives, action plans and a master calendar for the year of who does what and by when — may have various volunteer-related actions scattered throughout, or you may choose to have a separate section that focuses solely on volunteer plans.

A generic example of volunteer planning is shown here.

2012/13 Operational Plan
ABC Association

Volunteer Involvement Objectives

Objective No. 1: To manage the member recruitment committee (six members) and support them in generating 175 new members.

Objective No. 2: To coordinate two phonathons (fall and spring) that include no less than 35 volunteer callers. (Phonathon goal: 40 new members)

Objective No. 3: To coordinate and manage the golf classic planning committee made up of no less than eight volunteers. (Golf Classic goal: $40,000)

Objective No. 4: To manage the work of annual awards committee (five members).

Objective No. 5: To coordinate and manage the young professionals committee.

Volunteer Programs Calendar

MONTH	ACTION	RESPONSIBLE
June	Recruit phonathon co-chairs	Miller
July	Recruit phonathon callers (20-plus)	Miller
August	Recruit membership campaign chair; leadership	Gray
August	Young Professionals Committee meeting	Gray
September	Recruit member-get-a-member campaign volunteers	Gray
September	Board meeting — meet w/member recruitment committee	Gray
September	Hold fall phonathon	Miller
October	Member-get-a-member campaign kickoff	Gray
January	Board meeting — meet w/member recruitment committee	Gray
February	Recruit phonathon callers (20-plus)	Miller
February	Recruit Golf Classic chair; vice-chair	Fennel
March	Meet w/ Golf Classic chair, vice chair; recruit committee members	Fennel
April	Hold spring phonathon	Miller
May	Board meeting — meet w/member recruitment committee	Gray
May	Annual Golf Classic	Fennel

Advice to Create or Refine Your Membership Marketing Plan

Does your organization have a membership marketing plan? If not, you are likely being reactive rather than proactive in your marketing efforts.

"Without a plan, you are floundering around aimlessly. You risk losing time, money and opportunities," says Caroline Frankil Warren, manager of membership and chapter relations, Construction Specifications Institute (Alexandria, VA).

To develop the institute's marketing and recruitment strategies, Warren met with marketing staff, the department director, members and fellow staff. Through planning sessions:

- Marketing staff offered information about what they had done before, what was on the horizon, and ongoing input and review.

- The department director identified organizational goals and the desired direction/outcome.

- Members offered their best recruitment and retention strategies.

- Fellow staff shared ideas on new programs and products, and suggestions to make it all work.

With initial development stages of the plan complete, Warren says, they took these steps to create the plan:

1. **Drafted an initial outline** based on an organization's general marketing plan structure.

2. **Set organizational goals,** seeking ones relevant to their efforts (e.g., to increase membership, reach out to a particular population, publicize a new initiative or piggyback on a program from another department).

3. **Evaluated the plan,** analyzing factors that impact the campaign's success, including situation analysis; research on competition and competitive factors; industry analysis, noting current trends; organizational strengths, weaknesses (challenges) and opportunities.

4. **Determined strategies and how to achieve them.**

5. **Set a schedule** of when tasks needed to be done and by whom.

6. **Set a budget for the overall campaign as well as specific components,** with a component to monitor and measure results.

Warren shares the Construction Specifications Institute's membership marketing plan for its Member-Sponsor-a-Member Campaign, shown below and continued on p. 45.

Source: Caroline Frankil Warren, Manager of Membership and Chapter Relations, The Construction Specifications Institute, Alexandria, VA. E-mail: cwarren@csinet.org

—CSI Membership Marketing Plan, continued on p. 45 —

Content not available in this edition

Assembling an Effective Membership Marketing Plan

After holding a planning session for your marketing plan (see p. 44), you need to assemble that plan, says Caroline Frankil Warren, manager of membership and chapter relations, The Construction Specifications Institute (Alexandria, VA).

To create the best and fullest picture of what's going on in the industry and determine what your available resources are, what your timeline is and any new ideas, Warren says, be sure that you consider:

- **Situation/Organizational Analysis.** What is the current situation? What products and services do you offer to your target markets? What are your organization's major challenges? In what areas have you experienced significant successes? What are your greatest value propositions (where your organization provides value not found elsewhere)? Most importantly, what is the greatest goal you want to achieve for your organization with this initiative?

- **Competition.** What do competitors offer in terms of benefits and pricing? How do yours compare? Where do they lead the market? Where do you?

- **Industry.** What is happening in your industry and type of company (e.g., association, service oriented, etc.)? Do you see trends you should take into consideration? What key economic indicators do you need to keep in mind or success stories can you learn from?

- **Market/Customer Analysis.** Know your customers' income range, gender, occupation, primary interests, concerns, history with your organization, wants/expectations and if you are meeting those wants/expectations.

- **Developing Strategies.** Brainstorm the best strategies and how to achieve them. Where do you get information on marketing strategies? Ask your target market how they prefer to hear from you (e.g., e-mails or direct mail).

- **Schedules/Tasks.** Create a schedule for all you want to do or it won't get done. Allocating human and financial resources will assure that the jobs will get done. Breaking jobs down into several smaller tasks allows more people to get involved and gives you more support when one element goes awry and you need to fix it fast.

- **Budget.** Know how much you have to spend and how much you expect to raise. Then track how things are going compared against the metrics you have established with input from whomever is ultimately responsible for the bottom line.

Source: Caroline Frankil Warren, Manager of Membership and Chapter Relations, The Construction Specifications Institute, Alexandria, VA. E-mail: cwarren@csinet.org

Four Reasons to Craft a Membership Marketing Plan

Need more motivation to start crafting or updating your marketing plan? Know that with an effective plan, you can:

1. Look at your entire fiscal year and decide the best times to market to specific segments, working with your organizational schedule as well as the calendar year.
2. Budget using a plan, rather than randomly, allowing assignment of specific funds to specific projects. This gives a sense as to how much can be spent and for what.
3. Show others what you're doing, bringing greater input, buy-in and communication, plus maximization of efforts when one department piggybacks on another's efforts.
4. Better allocate human resources and manage staff workflow and other resources.

—CSI Membership Marketing Plan, continued from p. 44 —

Content not available in this edition

The Operational Plan: How to Create a Yearlong Membership Plan

MONITOR PROGRESS AND EVALUATE SUCCESS

The operational plan isn't intended as a one-time procedure that's followed prior to the onset of a new fiscal year and then gets no attention from that time forward. The plan should be reviewed individually and collectively by every member of your team on a regular basis throughout the course of the year. It should serve as your membership "instruction manual" all year long. An ongoing review of the plan will help to point out if particular strategies are on track or if other actions should be taken. Your written document will also allow you to evaluate what's working or not working and will provide valuable information as you prepare the subsequent year's operational plan.

Consider Holding a Midyear Staff Retreat

The obvious time for a staff planning retreat is just prior to a new fiscal year. But it can also be wise to hold a one- or two-day retreat mid-fiscal year.

A midyear staff retreat allows you to step back and evaluate where you are in relation to goals. It provides the opportunity to evaluate new members to date, recruitment efforts, effectiveness of specific retention strategies and more.

Staff can determine what strategies are working best and what adjustments are needed to meet or surpass annual goals. Since a midyear retreat focuses more on adjustments than creating a plan from scratch, it may also be a good time to discuss other key issues such as chapter relations, database management, volunteer involvement and more.

Are You Working Your Plan?

It's a significant accomplishment to prepare a written operational plan that outlines fundraising strategies for the year. But it shouldn't stop there. Be sure to work your plan as your fiscal year unfolds. Do that by:

✓ Referring to it at regularly scheduled staff meetings.

✓ Setting benchmarks throughout the year that compare the document's deadlines to actual results.

✓ Making notes on your operational plan that should be discussed or can be incorporated into next year's document.

Complete a Year-end Report

Whether your fiscal year ends in December or June or July, make time to complete a year-end written report that summarizes and analyzes key results. Both the process and final document will provide insight into planning future goals and objectives.

The report should include:

1. **Data on new member recruitment** — Total members recruited over/below goal, percentage increase/decrease over previous year, etc.

2. **Data on retention** — Number/percentage of retained members compared to previous year, number/percentage of member attrition, etc.

3. **Summary of member programs** — Members-only events, member offerings: educational, social, legislative, etc.

4. **Volunteer involvement** — Number of volunteers involved compared to previous year, types of volunteer involvement, total number of volunteer service hours compared to previous year, etc.

5. **Personnel issues** — Key performance issue, instances in which the staff/individuals exceeded or failed to meet expectations.

6. **Summary of shortcomings/disappointments** — Programs or recruitment/retention strategies that failed to meet expectations, internal/external factors impacting membership efforts.

7. **Summary of key accomplishments** — First-time initiatives, instances in which goals were met/exceeded, department/individual awards, individual performance accomplishments.

8. **Key recommendations** — Specific changes recommended for upcoming fiscal year.

Monitor Progress of Operational Plan at Staff Meetings

After you and your staff complete the important process of establishing a yearlong operational plan — including goals and quantifiable objectives, strategies, action plans and a master calendar — how do you monitor its progress throughout the year?

To stay on track, bring notebooks to regular staff meetings to provide a way to measure progress toward fundraising and other related goals.

The notebooks should include:

✓ A copy of your operational plan.

✓ Each meeting's agenda.

✓ Assignments that grow out of each meeting (with corresponding deadlines).

✓ Periodic reports (e.g., recruitment/retention updates, evaluation summaries of events, etc.).

Evaluate Your Website's Member Content

It's important to continually evaluate and refine your website, particularly as it relates to and reaches out to both members and would-be members.

Increasing numbers of nonprofit and association websites have several pages devoted to members.

Put some thought into all Web pages and features relating to members and prospective members to make it as easy as possible for website visitors to navigate your site.

Here is a sampling of website content and features (in no particular order) that reach out to members and would-be members alike:

- ❑ Benefits
- ❑ Networking
- ❑ Request for info
- ❑ Member categories
- ❑ Application procedures
- ❑ Bylaws, policies

- ❑ Dues structure
- ❑ Affinity groups
- ❑ Member chapters
- ❑ Contact information
- ❑ Member awards
- ❑ Member publications
- ❑ Educational opportunities
- ❑ Membership directory
- ❑ Member profiles
- ❑ Useful resources
- ❑ Member news
- ❑ Travel opportunities
- ❑ Achievements
- ❑ Members-only portal
- ❑ FAQ
- ❑ Legislative issues
- ❑ Member events
- ❑ Member testimonials
- ❑ Useful links
- ❑ Conference info
- ❑ Organizational profile
- ❑ Ways to volunteer
- ❑ Newsletter
- ❑ Annual report

Yearly Work Plan Puts Strategic Planning to Use

The National Association of the Remodeling Industry (Des Plaines, IL) had created strategic plans, but like countless other organizations, those documents often ended up on the shelf. "We needed a way to make sure the strategic plan was being utilized and the association's work was supporting it. That's how the work plan was born," says Nikki Golden, marketing and communications manager.

The work plan, she explains, is a tool that documents initiatives scheduled for the upcoming year, including the expected start and end date, budget, needed resources, evaluation metrics and assigned department and/or staff members of each.

The plan also provides space for ongoing status updates and, crucially, ties every project to one or more of the four key goal areas in the organization's strategic plan. "Basically, it ensures that the work we're doing actually furthers the mission of the association, rather than just supporting someone's pet project," says Golden.

Development of the yearly work plan begins with national committees, comprised of members, giving suggestions of initiatives for the coming year to staff liaisons. These suggestions are then taken to a two-day retreat where each is considered in terms of staff time and monetary resources required, as well as alignment with the strategic plan. Those that are judged worthwhile are fleshed out and added to the upcoming work plan.

Because the plan includes line-item budget figures for each project, it greatly assists the association's budgeting task force, which

receives a copy of the final document, says Golden. She also says that the clear responsibility it establishes for the execution of projects has helped improve staff and volunteer accountability.

The work plan is reviewed by staff members and the executive committee every quarter, providing a chance to update the status of projects and reorganize priorities, if needed. "It's not such a rigid tool that it can't adapt to changing circumstances," says Golden. "It's actually quite flexible, and could really be helpful to almost any type of group that takes input from many different sources."

Source: Nikki Golden, Marketing and Communications Manager, National Association of the Remodeling Industry, Des Plaines, IL. E-mail: Ngolden@nari.org

Content not available in this edition

Lightning Source UK Ltd.
Milton Keynes UK
UKOW01f0822020813

214783UK00006B/158/P